Anonymous

Moral and Philosophical Estimates of the State and Faculties of Man

And the nature and sources of human happiness. A series of didactic lectures. Vol. 4

Anonymous

Moral and Philosophical Estimates of the State and Faculties of Man
And the nature and sources of human happiness. A series of didactic lectures. Vol. 4

ISBN/EAN: 9783337070069

Printed in Europe, USA, Canada, Australia, Japan

Cover: Foto ©Paul-Georg Meister /pixelio.de

More available books at **www.hansebooks.com**

MORAL AND PHILOSOPHICAL ESTIMATES

OF THE STATE AND FACULTIES

OF MAN;

AND OF THE NATURE AND SOURCES

OF HUMAN HAPPINESS.

A SERIES OF DIDACTIC LECTURES.

VOL. IV.

LONDON,

PRINTED FOR B. WHITE AND SON, AT
HORACE'S HEAD, FLEET-STREET,
MDCCLXXXIX.

CONTENTS

OF THE

FOURTH VOLUME.

Eſtimate   Page

XXXI. *The Value of Learning.* — 1

XXXII. *The Value of more enlightened Times.* — 41

XXXIII. *The Value of Sufferings and Tribulations.* — 81

XXXIV. *The Value of a good Reputation.* — 117

XXXV. *Of Converſion from a Bad Courſe of Life.* — 153

XXXVI. *The Value of Human Happineſs itſelf.* — 183

XXXVII.

CONTENTS.

Estimate		Page
XXXVII.	Rules for rightly appreciating the Value of Things.	217
XXXVIII.	The Vanity of all earthly Things.	243
XXXIX.	Of the Moral Character of Jesus Christ.	273
XL.	Of the Imitation of the Example of Jesus.	309
XLI.	The Pastoral Office.	337

ESTIMATE XXXI.

THE VALUE OF LEARNING.

Happy are thy men, happy are these thy servants, which stand continually before thee, and that hear thy wisdom. 1 Kings x. 8.

THE VALUE OF LEARNING.

LEARNING, as well as the other prerogatives and advantages of mankind, is seldom judged of with strict propriety, is seldom taken for what it actually is. It has its panegyrists, who exaggerate its value; no less than its ignorant or haughty despisers, who refuse it the importance it deserves. Considered in its universal extent, to speak impartially, it has occasioned as much harm as good; has so frequently appeared under the most venerable aspect, and so frequently in the most ridiculous figure; and is compounded, in fact, of such a remarkable mixture of important and unimportant matters, that, as well in regard to the various sides it has, and the various effects it produces, as in respect to the various persons that profess it, it must necessarily undergo various and opposite sentences, one while deserving applause and admiration, and at another reproach and contempt.—Taken at large, it seems to have been more highly prized, and more honoured, in the early ages of antiquity, than in modern times: probably because it was less common; probably because the necessity and utility of it were in many respects more readily felt, and the helps it afforded were more indispensable; or, probably, because it wore a more venerable or more mysterious countenance, and was attributed to a sublimer origin. Accordingly, the queen that we read of, as coming from the wealthy Arabia, to converse with Solomon, had a very high opinion of its value. She left her throne, and

and her people, to hear and to improve by the wisdom, or, which in the language of those times is just the same, the learning of that monarch. Report had brought the fame of it into those distant regions, and had at once excited her appetence for novelty and instruction; and, on finding the truth of the matter to exceed even what report had made it, she exclaims in admiration, " Happy are thy men, happy are these thy servants, which stand continually before thee, and that hear thy wisdom!" Thus shewing that she preferred the erudition of Solomon before all his treasures, before all the splendour and magnificence of his court. And this judgement does her the more honour, as it is so very seldom that the great and mighty of the earth are impartial enough to do justice to eminent endowments of the mind, and to esteem them more than their own dazzling distinctions.

Let us, then, endeavour also to settle our judgement on the matter. Many of my audience are learned themselves, or make the works of the learned a chief part of their employment; and several have much connection and intercourse with that description of men: for both it is very important to acquire a due estimation of learning; and though I may possess but a small share of it myself, yet its properties, nature, and quality, cannot be utterly unknown to me; and it is more than possible that I may be able to pronounce the more impartially upon it, by renouncing, on that score, all pretensions to fame. Let us, therefore, investigate

The value of learning; and to this end,

First, make some remarks for properly stating its worth;

Then set that value in its proper light; and

Lastly,

Laftly, draw fome rules therefrom for our conduct in regard to it.

By erudition, or learning, I here underftand the whole circle of human fciences and knowledge, that do not immediately relate to the fatisfying the firft wants of nature; all knowledge and fciences that are generally more neceffary and peculiar to a certain clafs or body of men, than to mankind at large; whether, for the reft, they be diftinguifhed by diverfification and amplification, or by argument and method, be they of the hiftorical or philofophical fpecies, and of more or lefs general utility. Every one that addicts himfelf to any one clafs or kind of fuch knowledge and fcience, devotes the greater part of his time and faculties to it, and therein diftinguifhes himfelf above others, bears and deferves the name of a man of learning. And, for rightly appreciating the value of this learning, we muft make fome remarks upon it.

The first and most important, is this: the value that learning has is no otherwise, for the greatest part, due to it, than as being a means to higher aims, and not as an ultimate object itself; and this it has in common with the generality of the other privileges and advantages that relate to human happiness. Particular kinds of knowledge, certain branches of learning, have, indeed, in themselves, a value, an intrinsic and lasting value; but these are the fewest in number. Under this head we may, perhaps, reckon a great part of mathematical and astronomical knowledge, several of the deeper philosophical studies, and a part of our religious notions; whatever is eternal, unalterable, and everlastingly useful truth; all propositions and ideas that are of account in heaven as well as upon earth, among superior beings as well as among mankind; and though we may not completely possess such propositions and ideas, yet are we not totally destitute of them,

and

and they indisputably compose the most precious part of our knowledge. All that falls under this denomination besides has no value whatever, as an end, but only as a means. It is only so far respectable, and is only so far deserving of our esteem, of our attention, and our application, as it exercises the faculties of our mind, procures ourselves and others innocent and elevated pleasures, guides us in the track of truth, and facilitates the acquiring of it; gives scope to the activity of man, improves his outward welfare, provides for his conveniences, promotes his security, and helps him in the prosecution of his business, or procures him any other superfluous advantage. Hereto belong the generality of historical, the generality of mechanical and philological sciences, and the greatest part of the learning of the theologist, the physician, and the lawyer. They are only means, no more than implements, which we may attain, and forward certain good

good purposes in our present state; and which, when these ends are once obtained, lose absolutely all their value, and become useless, like old scaffoldings. That man, however, would think foolishly, who should suppose we might despise and reject them, while they are necessary to the prosecution of the building we are carrying on, before the structure be completely finished.

Hence spontaneously arises a second rule, of service to us in forming a right judgement of learning, and the several branches of it. It is this: the greater service and general utility it is of, the greater is likewise its value. Studies, absolutely unprofitable, when considered at least as means to farther views, are, indeed, no part at all of learning; many parts of it, however, are unworthy of the painful and indefatigable industry, the great application of time and abilities that are bestowed upon them. Many debase and weaken the mind

of

of a man, inſtead of elevating and ſtrengthening it; and benumb and contract his heart, inſtead of enlarging it, and quickening it to great and generous emotions. Many lead off ſuch as employ themſelves in them from the deſign of their creation, from their proper perfection, rather than facilitate them in the proſecution of it. Such learned attainments and occupations are, indeed, of but trifling value; often of much leſs value than the attainments and occupations of the artificer or the labourer; and he that makes them his principal employment has no right to complain, if he be neither more reſpected, nor more happy, than ſo many others of the unlearned, who trifle away their time like him, and diſſipate their powers No; he alone deſerves to be ſo, and that in a high degree, whoſe learning is, in any obſervable way, beneficial, and generally uſeful; who can give an account to himſelf, and to others, of what he has done and performed for the

advan-

advantage of his fellow-creatures; who effectually has kindled more light, and called forth more activity, in himself and about him; who has learnt to think and to live better himself; and has likewise, mediately or immediately, been the occasion that others think more justly, and live more prudently or happily.

A third circumstance, which falls under consideration in our researches into the real value of learning, especially in regard to particular persons, is this: the more discretion and true wisdom it has to accompany and guide it, so much the greater is its value. If learning allow room to pride, it soon degenerates into arrogance and tyranny; not unfrequently prevents its possessor from making greater progress in knowledge and science; often renders it unserviceable to others, or of but little use; and how very much must this detract from its worth! Still less value has the learning
which

which has no morally good influence on the mind and temper of the learned man; which allows him to think as meanly, and to act as corruptedly and foolishly, and as slavishly to follow the calls of his lusts and passions, as the ignorant and the unlearned; and in proportion as it procures but little real and durable advantage to himself, so much must this defect diminish its utility, in regard of others, and weaken its influence on human happiness. No; then alone does learning display herself in her native dignity, in her full splendor, and suffer none to doubt of her high value, when she appears in the company of modesty and wisdom; when she is not blind to her own infirmities and failings, and is not ashamed of her limitations; when she readily communicates herself to others; when she rather informs in the spirit of meekness, than decides in a haughty imperious tone; when she expresses herself in generous sentiments, by a beneficent and active

zeal

zeal for the cause of truth, of virtue, of liberty, of human happiness, and by an eminently wise, manly, virtuous behaviour, worthy of the enlightened man.

This pre-supposed, let us more closely examine wherein the real value of learning consists, and on what grounds it merits our respect.

Erudition is, first, mental perfection, and promotes mental perfection; and, if this be a real and respectable privilege of man, then must erudition be so too. The man of learning, who deserves that name, knows more of truth, sees farther into the principles and connections of truths, goes more surely to work in the investigation of them, and is therefore less liable to be imposed upon by appearance. His acuter sight takes in more objects; his trained eye explores much farther; he thinks more perspicuously, more profoundly, more justly,

than

than the generality of mankind can do; and who but muft confefs this to be a perfection, a prerogative? Allow that he fometimes miffes of his mark; allow that he is often expofed to the feductions of fophiftry and error; let the whole amount of the highly ufeful truths he has made out, clearly explained, or firft difcovered, be, comparatively, never fo fmall; yet he has been all that time exercifing his mental powers, learning to ufe them better, and with greater dexterity, and has thereby been advancing their effential and lafting perfection.—A thoufand things that we apply to, a thoufand things that relate to grammar, to the hiftory of nations, of nature and arts, and to other fciences, the knowledge of which comes under the article of learning, are in and of themfelves of no value at all, that a man fhould take the pains to ftudy and inveftigate them; but, not to mention the clofe connection wherein they frequently ftand with other

more

more important matters, they cannot be investigated and known, cannot be reflected on, methodized, combined, and applied; but we must, to that end, exercise our understanding, our acuteness, our wit, and our memory, and strengthen them by that practice; and this, undoubtedly, gives a great value and a utility to every kind of knowledge which we acquire, not barely in a mechanical and thoughtless way, but by consideration and reflection; it must give it a value and utility which will still abide by us, even when that very knowledge has vanished from our remembrance, and passed into complete oblivion. Thus, we all learn, in our younger years, a thousand things which we can turn to no account when we are advanced in life, and yet the learning whereof has been of great consequence to us, as we at the same time learn to think, to conclude, to determine, to revolve many subjects, to comprehend many, and connect many together.—Do not,

not then decline, O ingenuous youth, do not forbear to learn any thing that exercises thee in thought, if thou have time, and faculties, and opportunity for it, though thou perceive not the utility it may be of to thee, and though probably thou may not use it. The real, the greatest utility it can be of to thee is, that, at all events, thou wilt be the more rational and the wiser for it.—Therefore, let no man peremptorily despise him who, as it appears to him, pursues with too much earnestness, and too much industry, matters that, in and for themselves, are utterly insignificant, and promise no pleasure or advantage to any. All depends on the way and manner in which he employs himself about them. If he do it with intelligence and reflection, he may thereby learn to think as consecutively and justly as another, who busies himself on the most elevated objects. In this respect, even an inferior art, an ordinary trade, may be as profitable to the man that carries it on as learning itself. Both the one and the other are, in more than one confideration, nothing elfe but the fcaffold, whofe value muſt be adjuſted by the edifice to the building whereof it ferves.

Learning acquires, fecondly, a great value from the noble and never-ceaſing pleafure the inveſtigation and the knowledge of truth brings with it. So great as the pleafure of the traveller is, who leaves a perplexed and tortuous way, overgrown with thorns and briars, through a difmal and mazy foreft, for an even and luminous path, or after the darknefs of the night perceives the firft rays of the fun; fo great, and far greater ſtill, is the pleafure of the thinking man, on perceiving light, and order, and confiftency in his reflections, and can thereby proceed nearer to the knowledge of truth. And this pleafure the man of learning enjoys, not indeed abfolutely, but in an eminent degree. Every appli-

application of his mental faculties that is not totally fruitless, every extension of the sphere of his vision, every augmentation of his knowledge and inspections, every composure of his propositions and conceptions, every additional view he gets into the immense regions of truth, and every ray of light that falls upon his eyes, procures him this pleasure. And how diversified, how inexhaustible it is! Each stone, each mineral, each plant, each animal, each man, each part of man, the whole material and spiritual world, the visible and the invisible, the past, the present, and the future, the possible and the actual, the creature and the Creator; all charm, all employ the curiosity, the spirit of observation and inquiry of the thoughtful scholar; all guide him forward on the track of truth; all point out to him more or less of it; all shew him arrangement and harmony in the whole, and in the parts; all lead him to the prime, the eternal Source of Being, of life, of power,

power, of perfection; and by these very means procure him satisfaction, the purest, the noblest pleasure. A pleasure that often mounts to extasy, when he has overcome any material impediment that retarded him in his reflections, has obviated some difficulty that bewildered him, solved some knotty point on which he had exercised his perspicuity in vain; when he is enabled to fill up any considerable chasm in his knowledge, to exhibit a series of ideas with greater clearness, to comprehend more fully some part of human science, to find some important and fertile argument or exposition, to make any striking application, any profitable use of his knowledge, or to detect a trace of the truths that ensure him a remarkable progress in tilling the field he has chosen to cultivate. How often, and how amply, must these pleasures requite the naturalist, the astronomer, the geometrician, the philosopher, the chemist, and every other inquisitive mind, for all

its

its endeavours and toils in the search after truth! And how little has such an one to fear, lest the sources of these pleasures should ever fail, or the enjoyment of them be turned into disgust! No; here are fountains of pleasure that never cease, which flow through all times and all eternities, and are so much the more bounteous, the more pellucid and pleasant, the oftener and more copiously we draw from them. And must not learning, which procures us pleasures of this kind, be of great value?

Learning, thirdly, possesses a value, as a means whereby the general welfare of the whole community is promoted. How greatly have navigation and commerce been benefited by astronomical observations! how much have chemical researches contributed to the improvement and perfection of manufactures! how much are architecture, tactics, and every part of mechanical knowledge,

ledge, indebted to mathematics! What implement is there of the artist, of the artizan, or of the husbandman, that is not more or less improved and perfected by them? How many productions of nature are understood, enriched, and rendered useful to many important purposes, by the industry of the naturalist! What beneficial institutes in common and civil life, what conveniences in regard of lodging and furniture, of order and safety, of trade and traffic, are we not indebted for to learning, and particularly to geometry and the sciences related to it! How much is due to the study of law for peace and quiet, and to medicine for life and health, however great the inconveniences of the one may be, and the imperfections of the other! How much agreeable and useful knowledge, how many means of refined social pleasure, and noble entertainment, do we obtain from all these! Sources that diffuse themselves among all classes and condi-

conditions of men! Compare the situation of a country where ignorance and superstition prevail, with the state of another where learning and sciences flourish: how much more rudeness and ferocity, how much more imperfection and confusion, is in one than in the other! How many channels of industry, of art, of pleasure, of domestic and social felicity, run and disperse themselves throughout our happy country, bringing life and activity, profit and satisfaction, into all our borders! And how much more profit and pleasure of these various kinds may not the whole society promise itself in future from learning, since all men are at present far more disposed to render it more beneficial, and more serviceable, to all ranks and descriptions of persons than ever they were before!

Sound learning has, fourthly, a great value, as a means of security against all kinds of superstition and fanaticism. It
cherishes

cherishes and extends the lights of truth, which the offspring of darkness cannot well bear, and whom it often scares back into the obscurity from whence it sprung. It promotes clear thought, nice investigation, sagacious doubt, modest and dispassionate inquiry into the causes, the designs, and the connection of things. It shields us against the deceptions of the senses, the imagination, and the feelings; against the fallacious charms of the extraordinary, the wonderful, and the mysterious; against the dazzling vizor of a peculiar pensiveness and hidden wisdom, under which ignorance and fanaticism so often lurk. Wherever real learning and solid science lose their respect and influence, superstition is sure to rise upon their ruins, with all its lamentable and disastrous attendants, ignorance, dastardly fear, intolerance, and persecution, spreading terror, and thraldom, and misery of various kinds throughout a land. The appetence for knowledge never totally for-

sakes

sakes the human mind. If a man cannot employ it on regular and rational meditation, he endeavours to satisfy it by dreams and imposture. The invisible, the world of spirits, the future, is always of the highest importance to him. If, in his flights into that world unknown to him, he has not for his guide an enlightened and trained reason, but trusts to his own obtuse sensations or gloomy ideas; he is then liable to follow every bye-way, every devious track that offers; he runs the hazard of becoming the sport of every artful deceiver, or every dupe of imposture. But who can think on all the hurtful and ruinous effects of superstition and fanaticism, and not ascribe great praise to erudition, which is always counter-acting them, and setting bounds to their dominion?

Yet more. Considered as a support of religion, the learning which is not unworthy of that appellation, is of very great value;

value; and this must render it eminently dear to us, who profess and revere religion. The credibility and the divine authority of the christian doctrine rest, at least in part, on historical grounds; and these can neither be defended nor known, nor duly settled, without the help of learning. The understanding of the books which we hold for sacred, as the sources of this doctrine, implies a knowledge of languages, of antiquity, and of many other kinds within the province of learning. If we wish to see these doctrines defended, against the incredulous and the scornful; if we are desirous to have their reasonableness evinced, to have them purified from all human additions; more developed, and reduced to a connected and consistent whole; delivered in a manner suitable to the wants of men, and the requisitions of the times; and if we would have them likewise worthy of all acceptation to the deep-thinking man and the spirit addicted to doubt; would we

hope

hope to see them in security from all abuse; our hopes and desires would be vain, without the means of various sorts of learned knowledge; they can never be accomplished without the assistance of philosophical perspicacity, without an enlightened and habituated reason. Were it not for learning and solid science, religion would speedily degenerate into superstition and fanaticism. Whereas, the more flourishing and the more general they become, in any nation, or among a people, so much the greater light is diffused over religion; so much the more is it cherished in its native simplicity, and its majestic dignity, and so much the more general must its influence be on human perfection and happiness. Is religion founded on truth, and does it comprehend all truth? Then must every thing of necessity be favourable and helpful to it, by which the scrutiny and the knowledge of truth is conspicuously advanced. And what a value must accrue

from

from hence to erudition, in the fight of every man to whom religion and truth are no indifferent matters!

Lastly, learning, when it is and effects what it may and ought to be and effect, is an excellent preparative to the employment and pleasures of a higher condition after death. Much, perhaps even the greatest part, of our knowledge, and the sciences, as they are termed, will fall away as totally useless in the future life, as the toys and playthings of our childish years; yet must much of the rest still remain, such as are of a nobler kind, of eternal, unchangeable truth, of universal utility, and afford them, who take them with them into that better world, a more or less advantageous out-set, that will amply repay them for those they are deprived of. But, if this be no more than a prolusion of fancy, yet, in all cases, the scholar, who, in fact, supports that name, is always exercising his mental faculties

culties in a far superior degree; learns to inspect, to comprehend, and to combine more things together; raises himself in meditation farther above what is sensible and visible; habituates himself to more spiritual employments, and nobler pleasures; acquires a greater love for truth than for all things else; finds in the research and knowledge of it the purest delight; feels more sensibly the vanity and emptiness of all earthly things; feels himself more forcibly impelled towards the things that are invisible, towards such as are undecaying and eternal, towards God, the pristine source of all light and all truth, and proceeds on his way to his superior state with brighter prospects, with greater expectations; and must not this be a very suitable preparative thereto?

If, however, it be; if learning be an excellent habit and perfection of the human mind; if it procures a man real pleasure, and

and the noblest and purest kinds of pleasure; if it promotes, by various ways, the general well-being of human society; if it be an efficacious preservative from superstition and fanaticism; if it be a support to true religion, and a means of advancing it in the world; if it be adapted to fit us, in more than one respect, for our future superior state; then is it incontestable that it is of real and high value, that it may contribute, and actually does contribute, greatly to human happiness.

And, now, how are we to behave in regard to it?—The learned, as well as the unlearned, have many duties incumbent on them, in relation to this head. In conclusion, allow me to address a few words to the consideration of them both.

You, therefore, who devote yourselves to learning, or employ yourselves in it, take it for neither more nor less than it

really

really is. Prize and pronounce upon it, in the whole, as in its particular divisions, according to its proper worth; use it according to its true destination. Acknowledge that the generality of it, though serviceable, and in many respects useful and necessary, yet is not near so important as prejudice and self-love would probably allow you to believe. Acknowledge, and feel, and confess the imperfection, the uncertainty of all human knowledge and science. Frequently side with what you know, against what you do not and cannot know; what you know with assurance, against what is only hypothetical and probable; what you can actually make use of, against what is barely instrumental and matter of exercise, or even deception and error; what you may hope to carry with you into eternity, against what will be buried with you, and sink into the night of oblivion: and let all this teach you modesty and meekness. Let the sound intellect, the uncorrupted feelings

of

of the heart, the wisdom that is grounded on experience, and shews itself in an active and busy life, have ample justice. Reverence and pursue learning only so far as it makes you better, more intelligent, more wise, and more useful; and prefer the important to the less important, the serviceable to the less serviceable, as often and as much as your circumstances, and the duties of your vocation, will allow. Be not jealous of your acquirements, nor parsimonious of your information; rather study to incorporate all you know that is good and useful, every truth that is useful to mankind, by all the ways and means in your power, into the common stock of human knowledge. Let that greater light, which gladdens you, enlighten others also; and hide it not, out of slothfulness or fear, or self-interested motives, from the eyes of the world. Herein, however, take heed that you do not shake the foundations of morality, or weaken the bands of religion.

This, as the friend of mankind, you would not venture to do, even though you were perfuaded that the former were falfe and the latter chimerical; at leaft, not till you could furnifh your brethren with more ftable fupports to their faith and repofe. No; whatever promotes human perfection and happinefs muft be facred to you; and the true religion, which certainly promotes it in general, muft be moft facred.—Content not yourfelf fimply with being learned, but endeavour to be fo in a refpectable and amiable manner. Beware of the ordinary failings attendant on learning; of unfociablenefs, of mifanthropy, of defpifing and depreciating whatever lies not within your fphere, or relates to your purfuits. Be not haughty nor domineering; bear with the weak, the ignorant, the erroneous, in the fpirit of love; put them not to fhame, but convey to them inftruction; decide not on all things, and never decide without reafon; lower yourfelf to each man's capacity; hearken to their modest contradictions with calmness; and learn, even from the unlearned, as readily as you teach others. Respect the perceptions, the conclusions, the useful occupations of other men, though they should seem strange to you. Do honour, in fine, to learning, by the salutary influence you allow it to have on your character and conduct; display yourself more in generous sentiments and employments of general utility, than in diffusive science; and ever prefer doing to understanding, that is, virtue to knowledge.

And you, who do not belong to the class of the learned, despise not that which is foreign to you, or of which you have only a glimmering and faint conception. Rather esteem and prize that of which you are able to discern a little by a few reflections, sufficient however to shew you that it is of great and various service to you and to the whole community. Contemn

temn not the thing itself, because of its eventual abuses. Attribute not the faults and imperfections of the learned to learning itself. Do not require of men, who, in general, lead and are forced to lead a solitary life, and who seldom have a mind totally free, the vivacity, nor the polished breeding, nor the agreeable manners, nor the interest in all that passes, which you may expect from persons who live in the great world, and are present in all public diversions and pleasures. Respect the body of the learned, though perhaps all that belong to it are not respectable. Countenance and promote learning of every kind, by the esteem you shew to the learned, by the helps you afford them, by the assistance wherewith you facilitate their frequently expensive undertakings and pursuits, by the honour and rewards you bestow on their industry, and the service they render the public. But profit, likewise, by the greater light which learning diffuses around you.

Avail yourselves of it for rectifying and extending your knowledge, as far as is consistent with your calling and your other duties. But strive not after such learning, as in your station cannot be acquired but by the neglect of your most important occupations and affairs, and which, in the degree you would probably wish to possess it, would more confuse than settle you, would be of more harm than advantage to you. Neither pretend to an acquaintance with such kinds of knowledge and science which are either totally unknown to you, or of which you scarcely know more than the name; at most, have only some general notions. In many cases, it is far better to be ignorant, and not to be ashamed of one's ignorance, than to put up with superficial knowledge, and then to be as proud of it as if it were real learning.

Lastly, let all, both learned and unlearned, so think and so live as men sedulous

lous to promote the benefit of one and the same family; as members of one body, whereof one is the eye, another the ear, a third the hand, and a fourth the foot, and who are all equally neceffary to the fupport and well-being of the whole body, whereof none can difpenfe with any of the others. So fhall we all fulfill our duty, all worthily maintain our ftation, and reach the fuperior defign of our exiftence; all learn to love and efteem each other more and more, and each by means of the other become conftantly more happy.

ESTIMATE XXXII.

THE

VALUE

OF

MORE ENLIGHTENED TIMES.

———

Now are you light in the Lord: walk as children of light.   Ephef. v. 8.

LETTER TE XXXII.

THE

VALUE

OF

MORE ENLIGHTENED TIMES.

Now are you light in the Lord: walk as children of light.
Eph. 5.

THE VALUE OF MORE ENLIGHTENED TIMES.

THE times wherein we live are frequently called enlightened times; and, in fact, they are not absolutely undeserving of that epithet. Less ignorance in general prevails at present, less superstition and blind credulity, than in the days of our fathers. At present, undoubtedly, men reflect more upon morality and religious matters than perhaps they ever did before. There are now a hundred persons who employ themselves in reading, and thereby acquire some notions and science, for one that did so, I will not say

in

in the times of antiquity, but even at the commencement of the prefent, and in the courfe of the laſt century. Many kinds of knowledge are, at prefent, diffeminated amongſt all claſſes and conditions of men, which were heretofore confined to the learned. In our times a man is afhamed of many errors, many prejudices, many fuperſtitious and childifh opinions and ufages, which formerly were held facred by princes as well as their fubjects, by the noble as well as the vulgar. At prefent the purfuit of truth, and the free inveſtigation of it, are more general than before. Accordingly there actually is more illumination, there is a greater proportion of knowledge, there are more means and incitements thereto among mankind, whether they be near fo great and fo general as numbers pretend, or not.—But does this greater illumination give our times a real precedence above the foregoing? Are they actually more valuable on that account?

On

On this head there are various judgements, according to the point of view from which the matter is beheld.

Indeed this acceffion of light, particularly at firft, and before it be come to a certain degree of perfection, is productive of more or lefs harm. It excites doubt; it makes the faith of many weak perfons to totter; it puffs up the proud; it often begets fcoffers; it occafions at times fad feditions and difturbances; it will be mifufed by the wicked, for the purpofe of excufing and palliating their vices and follies; in fome refpects it promotes or favours a difpofition to luxury and magnificence, too great a propenfity to diffipation and public diverfions; it probably weakens and enervates many, by refining their tafte, and employing their mind to the detriment of their body; it feduces many to meddle with things quite out of their fphere, with which they have no concern whatever, and thereby by to neglect more important affairs; it frequently renders certain serviceable and useful institutions, methods, customs, and writings less effective, as people are enabled to spy out their defects and faults, but are not yet able to supply their places with better. All this is undeniable. And yet the greater proficiency of a nation in knowledge remains, notwithstanding, a real and respectable advantage; it is always far preferable to its opposite. The evils of the former are not general; they are at least but transitory, and will be far overbalanced by the good which is the natural consequence of this proficiency. And this is the matter I intend here to discuss. We are doubtless a people greatly enlightened, and we begin to enjoy the advantages of our proficiency. As christians, we are brought to the knowledge of truth; we should reason and live like men who profess the truth. Both as men and as christians, we are in possession of more means

of

of instruction and improvement than many other, perhaps than the generality of men and nations; we are already, then, capable of being farther enlightened than they; it, therefore, behoves us to conduct ourselves conformably to these privileges.

The gradual and insensible improvement of mankind is a natural effect of the dispositions and arrangements which God has established in the world, and the course he has prescribed to the human mind. As, in nature, the dawn succeeds the night, which likewise gives place to the shining day, and every creature feels itself produced anew to life, incited to the fresh expansion of its powers, and to proceed nearer to the design of its existence; so likewise the knowledge and sagacity of mankind are ever extending their circuit and advancing in evidence, and their minds are constantly striving after greater activity, after higher perfection, when the progress of the former and the endeavours of the latter are not impeded and limited by authority. This general proficiency in knowledge is therefore perfectly in the order of Providence, as a part of the plan laid down by God in his government of the world. It muſt, therefore, be good; it muſt have a real and great value, even though we ſhould not allow it. In this manner are we taught by religion to judge of it, and our reflections convince us that this judgement is true. For, what various and conſiderable advantages accrue from a more copious acceſſion of light to mankind, to the nation that has it to rejoice in!

Firſt, wherever it exiſts, it produces a far greater and more complete developement and application of the mental powers of man. This no man will deny. But is not this uſe, this exerciſe, this perfection of our nobleſt faculties, highly deſirable; and muſt it not be highly deſirable in regard

gard of all mankind? Is not the end of their creation, in effentials, the fame? Are they not, during this period of their exiftence, to rife from fenfual to rational creatures? Are they not all to think, juftly and truly to think, and to ftudy to raife themfelves more and more above the vifible and the prefent? Are they not all capable of continual improvement? Have they not all the fame obligations, capacities, and powers? Can the tenor of thefe obligations, the development and exercife of thefe powers, be bad and hurtful? Or are they only to be complied with, to be unfolded and exercifed by the learned, by men of fuperior ftations? Why then do all men poffefs them in common? Or is it right and fit that the delineation of thefe obligations, this developement, this exercife of the mental faculties, fhould be arbitrarily limited and controuled? Who may arrogate to himfelf this right over his brethren? Do not thefe limitations and circumfcriptions,

tions, so far as they are just or expedient, necessarily depend on the particular complection of persons, of times, of circumstances, on certain means, and the actual state of affairs? And if, in general, these limitations were more dilated, what mighty harm would ensue? Or is truth perhaps the exclusive property of the learned, or of the government, or of the opulent and noble? Is not, rather, every man ordained and called to the knowledge of truth? Is it not reputable and salutary to every man? Let it, alas! be liable to be misunderstood and misused by numbers! Are they always to misunderstand, always to misapply it? Does not the twilight bring on the morning, and that again the steady light of noon? Should there be then no twilight, lest any, deceived by its feeble rays, should slumber, or lose their way? Is, then, the night more favourable to the traveller than the dawn? Is error, is ignorance, always harmless? Are not the evils it is attended
with

with much greater, and more various, than those the misuse of truth occasions?—Certainly he that esteems and loves mankind, his brethren, he who understands their nature and appointment, will spread light around him whenever he can, and is unconcerned in the consequences it may produce; for this he knows for certain, that light is better than darkness. No; it is only the wish of the traitor, of the tyrant in the state and in the church; it is only necessary to the attainment of their despotic designs, that men should be kept in blindness and error, should be withheld from approaching the light, lest they should see through the veil of their flagitious intentions and actions. It is written, and may well be applied to this subject, "Every one "that doeth evil, hateth the light, neither "cometh to the light, lest his deeds should "be reproved." And for the same reason it is, that he hindereth others from coming to the light, as far as lieth in his power.

Farther. Where men are more enlightened, there is more complete and more elevated use and enjoyment of the beauties and blessings wherewith God has embellished our earth, and by which he has revealed to us his greatness and glory. What are all the beauties, all the wonders of nature, all its bounties and delights, to the unthinking man, who lives amongst an unenlighteued people! How little will they be observed by him! How much less will they be enjoyed in rational consciousness and chearful elevation of the spirit to God! How seldom used to the ends they are best adapted to promote! In vain do the heavens and the earth preach to him the glory of God, the Creator and Father of the world! Cold and thankless he sees them with barren surprize; he diverts himself with them, indeed, as a child is amused with the bright sparks he perceives in the firmament at night, and the variegated colours with which the face of the earth is adorned;

adorned; he tramples under foot, with equal indifference, plants and flowers, and creeping things; and takes no farther interest in them all, than as they bring immediate advantage or detriment to him. His belly cleaveth unto the ground, and so does his spirit also; he seldom raises himself above the visible and the present; and stands much closer allied to the beasts of the field than to spirits and superior beings. Confined to the narrow circle of his terrene occupations, and the pleasures of sense, he leaves the sun and the moon and the stars to rise and set, the parts of the day and the seasons of the year to perform their stated revolutions, one wonderful appearance in nature to follow on another, without asking himself a single question about the causes, the designs, and the connections of these things; without rejoicing in them with consciousness and reflection; without being sensible to the greatness of God, to the bounty of his heavenly Father, and to his own happiness. And, truly, is this a state, this the behaviour worthy of a man? Does he thus maintain the post he fills as a rational creature, as the priest of nature, upon earth? Does he thus, indeed, reach the end for which God has encompassed him with so many beauties and blessings, with so many indications of his power, of his wisdom, and of his goodness, and granted him a mind to understand them, and a heart to feel them? And must not a greater abundance of light, which promotes this end, and opens to every not absolutely inattentive man at once the book of nature, and his own eyes to peruse it, be conformable to the will of the Creator, and to the nature of man? Must it not possess a real and great value?

The greater abundance of light, thirdly, delivers mankind from many of the degrading and oppressive shackles of superstition and servile fear. Allow, if we must allow it, that the lower and more numerous clafs of men require narrower boundaries and a tighter rein, if we would have them not abufe their faculties, nor neglect their duties: yet to this end neither fuperftition nor thraldom are neceffary, and evils that could only be guarded againft by fuch means would ceafe to be evils. No; even in this refpect we are not permitted to do evil that good may come. Superftition and bondage far too deeply degrade mankind; obfcure by far too much the image of God, his Creator, in him; keep him by much too diftant from the end of his being; are much too manifeftly at ftrife with his perfection and happinefs; for us not to prize, revere, and promote, as matters of the higheft moment, whatever can fecure or deliver him from them; and this a greater degree of light undoubtedly does. It diffipates a thoufand and a thoufand idle terrors, which formerly perplexed and tormented mankind; a thoufand kinds of impofture posture and errors which formerly held them in the severest bondage. It is only by such illumination, that the childish and prejudicial belief in spectres, in conjuration and witchcraft, in supernatural arts and sciences, in the authority and influence of evil spirits, is weakened and destroyed. And how much does this belief dishonour and disgrace the man, the christian, the worshiper of the only true God! How contradictorily did it cause him to think, and how inconsistently and foolishly to act! How often did it deprive him of all spirit to good actions! and how oft did it seduce him into shameful transgressions! What cruel perturbations tormented him on all sides, and how seldom could he rejoice in existence!—And how can true religion and solid piety find place, where superstition and servile dread prevail! But is true religion and solid piety, are filial love to God and filial satisfaction in him, is the rational and chearful enjoyment of life, the heritage of of only a selected few, or, at most, of some ranks and classes of men? Are they not the portion of mankind, as men; of the christian as a christian? Can their sway become ever too general, or be too firmly established? Can their influence on human conduct and on human happiness ever be too great? And, if that be not possible, who can deny the value of that enlightening, whereby they are so much advanced, or who shall arbitrarily prescribe it bounds? No; whoever does so, must himself, though probably he will not confess it, must himself doubt of the truth, and hold the grounds of religion to be very fluctuating and uncertain, or the fear that either the one or the other might suffer thereby would never enter his mind.

The more the times are enlightened, the more favourable they are to true religion. Indeed, not to every religion; not to the appendages by which even the true religion

gion has been encumbered and disfigured. These must assuredly by degrees fall off, where greater lights and free investigation obtain. But is this to be set to the account of profit or loss? Is it to be dreaded or desired by the friend of truth, and the friend of mankind? Is it not the additions of men which so much restrain and enfeeble the effects of true religion, that render what is called religion so unproductive, and to many even hurtful? Examine the religion of an unenlightened nation, of a nation where implicit faith prevails. In regard of the generality of its professors, is it any thing more than a string of sentences repeated by rote, a round of ceremonies, lip-service, and self-deceit? The grossest conceptions of the Deity, with a low, servile, and childish conduct towards him; the most superstitious notions of the miraculous effect of certain words and solemn rites and outward actions, and a totally blind confidence in these words and rites

and

and actions; a tormenting scrupulosity about indifferent things, and inconsiderate disregard to the most important; slavish fears and idle hopes; zeal without knowledge; faith without virtue; devotion without philanthropy; austere observance of arbitrary impositions and injunctions, and a general relaxation of indispensable obligations: this is, generally speaking, the religion of every nation where men shun the light, and refuse it admission to the human mind. And is, then, such a religion indeed so respectable, so salutary, that I should esteem it inviolable and unimprovable, that it must be secured against all free investigation, and concealed from the light? Admit, to our sorrow, that this investigation, that this light, may be attended by unbelief in one person, a disposition to cavil in another, and in a third indifferency. Will this be the fruit of them in all men, must they have these effects for ever? Will they not produce in
many,

many, will they not probably in time be productive of sound knowledge of the truth, and of inward conviction of it, in the generality of men? And do we not find, that where darkness and ignorance prevail, as much at least of unbelief, of doubt, of indifferency in regard of the most essential points, and perhaps still more? And then, if the number of the outward professors of religion were reduced, what would it lose by the defection of such false or cold friends? Would not the rational faith, the belief founded on discussion and conviction, of the rest, be productive of more benefit, promote real virtue and happiness in them and around them, so much the more?—No; true religion needs never be shy of the light; and he that extends this, is at the same time extending the reign of happiness and virtue. The christian, says one of the first promulgators of christianity, is a light in the Lord; if, then, he would maintain this

cha-

character, then muſt he behave like a child of light, as a friend and promoter of it.

Enlightened times are, fifthly, favourable to virtue. It is true, that proficiency in ſcience and virtue do not always proceed with an equal pace. Nay, the former may eventually be detrimental to the latter: but aſſuredly not upon the whole. The virtue of the cœnobite, the virtue of the hermit, the virtue of the fanatic of every denomination, if any will call them by that name, are confeſſedly ſufferers by the diſſemination of knowledge; they are plants that thrive better in the boſom of darkneſs than by an influx of light. But certainly not the virtue of the citizen, of the ſenſible man, of the true chriſtian! What is virtue, if it be not founded on ſcrutiny and choice, but is the effect of neceſſity, of conſtraint, of ſervile fear, or merely of mechanical habit? Does it deſerve that venerable name? Is it indeed conſiſtent with itſelf?

itself? Can it have much inward strength and firmness? Does it confer any honour upon a man? Will it guide and govern him in concealment as well as in the eyes of the world, in common and familiar life as well as in the solemn offices of devotion or in civil affairs, in the enjoyment of liberty and pleasure as well as under the heavy hand of power, or in the midst of misfortunes? No; only the virtue that is thoroughly deserving of that name is a daughter of light, the result of plain research and intimate conviction, which is founded on a true knowledge of our nature, our present and future appointment, our conduct towards God and man, towards visible and invisible things. She alone is always equal; rests upon firm, immovable foundations; is ever the same in all times, in all places, in all conditions; exalts and dignifies whatever a man does; accompanies him wherever he is, and never deprives him of her counsel and support.

She

She alone wants neither outward forcible means, nor mechanical incitements, and finds in herself inducement and ability enough for doing constantly what is right and good, what is fair and noble, what is for the best in every event. Admit that we may suppose such a virtue where there is no great degree of scientific improvement: but must not whatever promotes and extends it be, sooner or later, favourable to it? How much more sensible and tender must the moral sense, the conscience of the enlightened man, be! How many more arguments, and how much higher and nobler arguments must he bring forward to his mind, as often as he has to chuse between good and evil, or between good and better! How much farther must his sight pierce into the remoter consequences of his undertakings and actions! How much more accurately must he apply the general rule of his conduct to every particular circumstance; how much more

easily

easily is he able to connect the present with the future! How much more nicely will he discriminate semblance from truth, what has only the looks of virtue, from virtue herself! How much less will he be satisfied with only the inferior degrees of it! No; fear not, O ye friends of Virtue! that the respect of your friend can be lessened by this means among mankind, or her empire contracted, by your enlargement of the kingdom of light. Truth and virtue are sisters, they are inseparably connected together; the true votaries of the one are also true votaries of the other; the prevalence of the latter is so much the more unrestrained, by how much the former is extended and advanced; their sovereignty is one and the same.

In enlightened times, sixthly, men are more sociable, are brought nearer together, connect themselves more intimately with each other, and by more various ties.

Their

Their manners will be rendered milder, more agreeable; their conversation more entertaining; their intercourse more pleasant and affectionate; their desires and endeavours to ingratiate themselves with each other will be greater. The higher and lower stations and classes of men are less dissevered; they intermingle more, have more common pursuits and pleasures; and thereby the pride of the one will be abated, and the decent confidence of the other encouraged. Social pleasures will be multiplied, refined, and dignified in enlightened times. They will, in part, be derived from sources that are absolutely shut up to an unenlightened people. The history of nature and art, of the generations of men and the planting of nations, personal and foreign experiences and observations, in one case, furnish the richest and most ample materials for discourse, for a useful as well as agreeable exercise of the understanding, the discernment, the wit, the imagination,

for

for the maintenance and support of rational chearfulness and mirth. Every man is more earnest to present himself on the most favourable side, to exchange information of one kind for information of another, and to impart as much satisfaction and delight, as to receive. And must not this be a covetable privilege above the condition of unenlightened men, whose manners are generally rude and ferocious, whose pleasures are altogether sensual, whose diversions are merely riotous and noisy, whose views are to the last degree contracted, whose mental faculties are undeveloped and unexercised, and whose deportment is seldom agreeable; but much oftener arrogant and disgusting? —And must not the advantages of the former be in perfect harmony with the intentions of religion and nature? Is it not the aim of both to unite men progressively more, to inspire them with more and more love and esteem for each other, to render them continually more useful and agreeable

to

to one another, ever more inclined to unfold their mutual capacities and powers by social wants and propensities, by social businesses and pleasures, by all these means to improve the sum of their social happiness, and thus constantly to approximate them to the purposes of their existence, as one single closely connected family of brothers and sisters, dwelling together and making each other happy? Allow, then, that this greater sociality, this refinement of manners, this intermixture of ranks, this extended action and activity, may have their unavoidable inconveniences and disadvantages. Allow that they often degenerate into vanity and frivolity; allow that they frequently are accompanied by dissimulation and falsehood; grant that they dissipate too much the attention and the faculties of many; let it be allowed that at times they infringe on the rules of strict propriety. Upon the whole, they always effect by far more good than harm, occasion far more happiness than misery; are always a step in advance towards the perfection of human nature, an emollient and sweetener of the hardships of this terrestrial life.

Enlightened times are productive of still more good. The stations and affairs of men are more dignified; and therefore we have fresh incitements to fill more worthily the former, and better to transact the latter. Indeed the first beams of stronger light often produce quite contrary effects. The youth who has acquired some knowledge, and thinks he has refined his taste, may easily be induced thereby to despise the condition and calling of his forefathers, and to neglect its concerns, as thinking himself capable of greater and more elevated affairs. But in this evil, which only obtains in particular occurrences, and for the most part is soon remedied by the punishment that follows it, or by maturer judgement,

is

is this to be compared with the general and lasting evils which the defect of improvement in this respect naturally brings on? How deplorable is the moral condition of a people, where no one sees farther than the contracted sphere of his own art, his own work, or his own trade; where none is interested about what happens otherwise than as it regards himself; none thinks on the connection of the whole, and on his own influence upon it; none acquires any knowledge but what he absolutely must; none ventures to tread out of the road which his sires and grandsires trod before him; where every one works and employs himself more by compulsion than inclination; where every one is only animated by self-interest, and guided by custom; and if he has any more time or means than what his mechanical labours require, he knows not what to do with either, and loses them both! But, on the other hand, let light but once have made considerable

progress amongst a people; let men of all classes and conditions have learnt to reflect more; let them have acquired greater knowledge of their appointment and that of their brethren, be better acquainted with the wise œconomy of God upon earth, with the true value and coherence of things; be better informed in what real honour and dignity, in what perfection and happiness consists; let them set about whatever they undertake and do, less mechanically, with more rational consideration; how quickly will every man learn to prize his station, to understand the needfulness and utility of it, to carry on the business it requires in a nobler manner, to enjoy the benefits it procures him more rationally and chearfully, and to be in all respects more useful to the community! And how much more will he thus promote his satisfaction and his mental perfection! How differently will he find himself repaid for his diligence and industry! When can he be deficient in resources

sources of useful employment, even out of his peculiar circle, and of elevated recreation! How important, how agreeable must the labours and affairs of the countryman, the artist, the merchant, the artizan, by this means become, when he prosecutes them with a liberal mind, free from prejudices, with an enlightened reason, and accustomed to reflection, and feels the value of all he does! And how considerably will all be gainers thereby! Indeed we are still very far short of this degree of light. But, if it be desirable, then must likewise the way that leads to it be good, though it be beset with many obstacles. Even the best field is not free from every kind of weeds; much less that which has so long lain fallow, which has scarcely been begun to be tilled, and which is sown with grain that cannot be perfectly sound and unmixed.

More enlightened times are, lastly, preparative to that better state which awaits us after death; and this so surely as, in that state, knowledge of truth and spiritual perfection are the foundation of our superior felicity. I am sensible that at present we can frame but very dark and indefinite conceptions of our future state, and can know but extremely little of the peculiar occupations and pleasures of it. I am, however, firmly persuaded of this, as I have observed in a former discussion, that the greatest part of our knowledge, considered as knowledge, of whatever species or kind it may be, must there be obliterated as totally useless; and that, in this respect, the enlightened man, the man enriched with all the treasures of learning, will have no great advantage over the unlettered and ignorant. But this is very certain, that our future life is coherent to the present, that it is a sequel of it, that the degree of inward perfection we here attain will denote the point of perfection of which we shall there be capable. This is very certain, that in that,

as

as well as in the present state, we shall think, shall strive to find out truth, shall advance in the knowledge of truth; that we shall do all this as men, and that it will be so much the more easy or difficult for us to do, that we shall advance more rapidly or more sluggishly, as we have more or less exercised ourselves in them here. And, if the case be thus, then must every thing that trains us in thought, every thing that promotes inward spiritual perfection, then must likewise greater proficiency in lights, be preparatives to that superior state, as the strongest incitement and best means thereto; then must enlightened times have a real and great value in this respect also. Are we already, in this world, the children of light; do we here already live in the kingdom of light; are we eager to imbibe every ray of it, however feeble; so must we become the fitter for its brighter influx, for its perfect splendor, in a better world!

This will suffice for displaying the great value of a considerable progress in luminous acquirements, and place it beyond all doubt. May I be allowed to adduce from it a few admonitions in regard to our conduct?

If you are sensible to the worth of this advantage, then use all diligence to turn the portion you are blessed with of it to the most profitable account; and let it, by your means, be productive of that good it may and ought to produce. The more enlightened the times and the men, in which, and among whom you live; so much the more must you be ashamed of all ignorance, of superstition, of blind faith, of thoughtlessness and indifference in respect to matters which it behoves all men, and consequently you, to know. Therefore, shut not your eyes against the light that shines around you. Walk not in darkness, since the day begins to appear. In regions

regions where all is dark, where ignorance and superstition prevail without controul: there no man indeed need be ashamed of being ignorant and superstitious, to feel his way through the gloom, and to stumble or to fall at every step he takes; for there one is as weak and as wretched as another, and yet believes none to be either wretched or weak. But, to prefer darkness to the light that beams upon our eyes; to stumble and to fall in a path enlightened by the sun, as though it were shrouded in the deepest night; to remain still ignorant and superstitious amidst all the means to knowledge and a rational faith; this indeed degrades a man, this renders him grossly criminal. And this, sirs, will be more or less the case with you. The night is far spent, may we likewise exclaim to you, with an apostle, the night is far spent; the day is at hand, the dawn has already appeared: it is high time to awake out of sleep. The time is over and gone, when
free

free reflection and inquiry was a crime, and implicit belief meritorious: none of you, except by his own fault, can be deficient in means and inducements to reflection, to research, to the augmentation and improvement of his knowledge. Avail yourselves of these means and inducements, use them like men endowed with reason, and as christians who are rouzed to freedom. Remain not supine on the couch of tradition, in the place where prejudice and former instruction left you, as if they were the boundaries of all human knowledge. Implicitly follow no human leader; from children proceed to be men, who thinking for themselves, go alone, and have learnt to proceed with a firm and steady step along the path of truth. To think and act upon thoroughly tried and sure principles; constantly to be striving after greater light, after farther certainty; to love truth above all things, and to receive it with an open heart, without regard to prevailing opinions

and

and outward circumſtances, as it is exhibited to you; is what muſt diſtinguiſh you from leſs enlightened men, and your times from the times of ignorance and darkneſs.

Farther. If you confeſs the great value of enlightening a nation, then let every one promote it according to his ſtation and in proportion to his abilities. Particularly you who are teachers of the people, or are farther advanced in knowledge than the reſt. But do it with that prudence and affection, which ſhould guide and animate us in all our affairs, and moſt in the moſt important. Every man is not capable of every truth. Every manner of producing and of diſſeminating even the moſt generally uſeful truths, is not the beſt. Few perſons are ſtrong and liberal enough to comprehend and adopt and rightly uſe truths hitherto unknown to them, or even a confiderable part of them. Too bright a diſplay of light, that does not make its approaches

approaches by degrees, but is suddenly intromitted in all its force, frequently dazzles more than it enlightens. In the moral as well as in the natural world, the transition from the darkness of night to the full blaze of noon must come on by degrees, if we would have mankind enjoy that light, and not be forced to shut their eyes against it. Take heed then not to favour the mistakes of any, even of the wise; and still more, not to confess and to teach them as truths. This is a horrible act of high-treason against truth, and debases every man that does so, even if he do it in really good intentions. But do not therefore directly contend against every error; do not furiously attack every thing that either is or appears to you to deserve that name: otherwise, you may at the same time shake the grounds of truth, which are often in more than one respect connected with error, and thus prevent its admission into the heart. As little may you venture to

bestow

bestow or to obtrude every truth, without distinction or exception, on every human mind. As every kind of grain will not flourish in every soil, so neither is every truth adapted to the comprehension of every man. Even the proper field requires previous cultivation before it can be sown with any reasonable expectation of a copious harvest.—If you would contribute to the enlightening of your brethren, begin by setting their attention and curiosity in motion; bring them to the sentiment of their imperfections and spiritual wants; induce them to think, and assist them in their thoughts; conduct them into the footsteps of truth, and remove the principal impediments out of their way; make them see what they already know and believe in a clearer light, or understand it with greater perspicuity, and thus accustom them to clear and calm reflection, which will incite an eagerness after greater light. By this means you will best carry on your attacks

against

against levity and slothfulness of mind, sensuality, indifferency in religious matters, the low, servile fear of men, false scrupulosity, hypocritical piety; and thus stop up the springs of error and superstition. Render truth respectable and amiable to every man, by the modesty and meekness with which you deliver it, by the hilarity and quiet with which you possess and display it, by the influence it has on your temper and manners. Recommend and disperse all good writings, that promote reflection among mankind, and are favourable to the knowledge of truth. Pay particular attention to the instruction and formation of young persons, and thus lay the foundation of greater proficiency for the next generation.

In fine, if you confess the value of greater illumination, and actually enjoy the benefits of it, then walk, as we are exhorted to do in the scripture, as children of light. Conduct yourselves as men who

profess

profess the truth, and are become wife and free by the knowledge of it. Let its light not merely have an influence on your mind, but let it govern your heart and actuate your whole behaviour. Live as you think. Exhibit your character as much, and even more, by generous sentiments and good deeds, than by just conceptions. Light, that does not at once animate, warm and fertilize, knowledge that does not make us wifer and better, is of no great value, is frequently more prejudicial than useful to us. Your progress in knowledge must be not so much the ultimate object, as means to higher aims; means to purer virtue, to greater perfection and happiness. The truth that prevails in your ideas must likewife prevail in your feelings, in your views and endeavours, in your difpofitions and actions, in your whole behaviour. Only by so judging in every concern, by being so difpofed in every circumftance, and by so acting in every occurence, as the nature

of

of it requires, and is confiftent with your correlative fituation, will you advance towards perfection, and improve your fimilitude to the deity, your fupreme and eternal model; only thus the knowledge of truth can and will become to you a never-failing, a conftantly augmenting fource of happinefs and blifs.

ESTIMATE XXXIII.

THE VALUE OF SUFFERINGS AND TRIBULATIONS.

No chastening for the present seemeth to be joyous, but grievous: nevertheless afterward it yieldeth the peaceable fruit of righteousness unto them which are exercised thereby. Hebrews xii. 11.

THE VALUE

OF SUFFERINGS AND TRIBULATIONS.

GOD loves his creatures of the human race. This all nature proclaims aloud. This is declared by all the capacities and powers that God has given us, all the arrangements he has made in the moral and the phyſical world. Happineſs is our real, our whole appointment; the deſtination of all that exiſts and lives, and is ſuſceptible of happineſs. To this end has he made us; to this end has he given us this part of his dominion for the place of our abode, and embelliſhed it with ſo many beauties and bleſſings; to this end has he placed us in the various connections wherein we stand with the material and the spiritual world. He has likewise excited in us all a thirst, an ardent thirst after happiness; and how is it possible that he, the all-gracious, should have raised in us this thirst, and not have furnished us with the means of assuaging it!—No; we are surrounded on all sides with sources of pleasure and delight, inviting us to enjoyment, no less diversified than copious, and which we cannot altogether exhaust, nor each of their various kinds.

And yet man, this creature so beloved of God, and so evidently ordained to happiness, frequently meets with grievous afflictions; and no one yet of all our race has ever passed his life without having had them, more or less, to contend with. Are then these afflictions at strife with our destination? Do they block up our way to felicity? Do they annihilate the gracious designs of our Creator, the plans of almighty

mighty goodnefs? No, that is impoffible; even thefe afflictions muft tend to something good, muft poffefs a certain value, muft contribute to the advancement of our happinefs: otherwife God, who loves us with paternal tendernefs, and would have us happy and joyful as his children, certainly would never allow them to befall us.

And thus the matter ftands. Even fufferings and forrows are good; they are benefactions of our heavenly Father. They are means, harfh and unpleafant indeed, but efficacious and falutary means, for our purification, our amendment, and our higher perfection. They lead us a rough and doleful way, a way moiftened with tears, and the fweat of our brows; but a way that terminates in happinefs. Of this our own reafon and experience will not permit us to doubt; and the facred books confirm what they teach us, in a manner the moft exprefs. No chaftening, fays the

apoftle

apostle Paul, for the present seemeth to be joyous, but grievous: all severity is repugnant and disagreeable to us so long as we feel it. Nevertheless, afterward it yieldeth the peaceable fruit of righteousness to them which are exercised thereby: in the sequel it produces the best effects to them who allow themselves to be corrected by it, by rendering them good and virtuous persons. It was no less a personage than a king who said, "It is good for me that I have been afflicted, that I might learn thy statutes." And the apostles of Jesus, in their own name and in that of their fellow-christians, glory also in tribulations, knowing that "tribulation worketh patience; and patience, experience; and experience, hope; and hope maketh not ashamed." Let us then learn to take the disasters and tribulations of our lives, no less than the proper blessings and joys of them, for what they are and may become, and to apply them to the advancement of our happiness! My design is in this discussion to give some direction to your thoughts upon them.

Sufferings and tribulations have no value as an ultimate object, but only as means. They are not in and of themselves either good or wholesome, but only in regard of their effects. Sufferings are and must ever continue to be sufferings; disagreeable, painful sensations. Tribulations are and must ever remain tribulations; accidents and occurrences that are adverse to our nature, and hostile to our views and desires. While they are present, we think them unpleasant and grievous; and this, of themselves, they actually are. They are medicines, bitter medicines, which are not prescribed on account of the pleasantness of their taste, but only as good against disorders, and which probably we must be plagued and tormented with a long while before we are completely restored. They are exercises that are enjoined us, not on their own account, but for the fake of their effects. The fchools, confidered as fchools, have no great value. It is not the reſtraints they impoſe on our liberty; it is not the toilfome application they at one time induce and at another compel us to exert; not the chaſtiſement they beſtow on the inconſiderate fcholar, for his puniſhment and correction, that make them defirable. It is only the good confequences of thefe hard reſtraints, of this laborious affiduity, of this grievous chaſtening: only the uſeful knowledge, the better difpoſitions, the good habitudes, we thereby acquire, that give its whole value to every thing we do and fuffer there. So alfo fickneffes, misfortunes, loffes of goods and honours, loffes of patrons and friends, the failure of plans and undertakings, poverty, humiliations, perfecutions, and whatever elfe oppreffes and afflicts mankind, have only fo far any real worth, as by their means

means we become wiser, and better, and happier.

Hence it naturally follows, that they acquire this value only by the use we make of them. Not every man to whom medicine is administered, or who voluntarily takes it of himself, will thereby be healed. There must be vital powers yet remaining in him; he must not on purpose hinder and diminish the effects of the medicine he has taken; he must do or abstain from many things, which at other times he need not do or forbear, and so frame his whole conduct as is befitting his present condition. Not every one who frequents the schools, and allows himself to be instructed or is forced to be taught, will learn what they are adapted to teach. Many a one will leave them as ignorant and unqualified, probably more corrupted and vicious, than he was before. It is only the attentive, the studious, the obedient scholar,

who

who willingly imbibes inftruction and profits by difcipline, that returns from them enriched with the treafures of wifdom, and bleffes the man that entered him there. If we would have fufferings and tribulations to be of real value to us; then we muft ufe them aright; we muft account them for what they are; muft confider them in their dependency on God and his will; muft reflect upon them, fee them on their moral fide, attend to the defign of them, and conduct ourfelves in all refpects according to our fituation, as it is altered by them.

In fhort, fufferings and tribulations have comparatively no greater value than as they fnatch us from the dangers of an uninterrupted profperity, and teach us what that could never inform us of, or lead us to a point of wifdom and virtue to which profperity could never conduct us. On this principle, they are not neceffary to all men in the fame kind and to the fame degree.

gree. There are children who may be educated by pure affection; there are others that require a stricter discipline. The former have a tender and sentimental heart; feel the whole value of every kindness shewn to them; think nobly; and find no duty, no sacrifice, too painful whereby they may testify their gratitude to their benefactors, their friends, their tutors and guides: the latter sort are obstinate, selfwilled, and perverse; are by fare less tractable, much harder to be governed, and therefore require more forcible suggestions, must be often feelingly chastised, before they can be brought to submission and obedience. So likewise there are men of generous and noble souls, whom prosperity neither dazzles nor hardens, neither seduces them into folly, nor sinks them in vice; who find, in every benefit they receive from the hand of God, fresh incitement to justice, and fresh ability to beneficence; and who, thoroughly impressed with the love of God

and

and the love of man, require no other motives to make the beſt, the moſt generally uſeful application of all that they are and have. But, poſſibly, there is a much greater proportion of ſuch as are not to be led by uninterrupted ſucceſs, who would run the riſk of loſing all ſentiment of duty and virtue, all regard for religion, and all the feelings of humanity, and fall by little and little into the moſt abandoned profligacy: and, if theſe perſons are ſnatched from this danger by ſufferings and tribulations; if by their means every deadened ſentiment to what is beautiful and good be reſtored to motion; then certainly muſt ſufferings and tribulations be to them of far greater value than the moſt flouriſhing proſperity.

And thus in fact it is. And, to convince ourſelves of it, we need only proceed to examine a little more circumſtantially what it is that gives human ſufferings and tribulations this value, or wherein it conſiſts, and

and how they contribute to advance our happiness.

Sufferings and tribulations are, in the first place, much adapted to lead a man to serious reflections on himself, on the ends of his being, on his condition, and the way to happiness, to imprint those reflections on his mind, and actually to set him forward on that way. How rarely are these reflections made amidst the dazzling splendour, amidst the confused noise, the dizziness, the deceitful charms, the intoxication, that commonly attend on prosperity! how seldom there can serious thoughts obtain a hearing! how quickly are they scared away by the ostentation of vanity, the scoffs of the wanton, and the voice of the flatterer! how seldom there does a man retire to himself! how easily does he overlook and forget all his inward defects, all his spiritual wants, in the possession and enjoyment of so many outward
advan-

advantages! how readily does he there exchange reality for appearances, confound what he is with what he has, and lose sight of himself and his proper felicity amidst the enchanting visions that float upon his mind!—But, when the scene changes; when all these shining images disappear from his view; when the companionable buffoon, the scoffer, the flatterer, the false friend, forsake his unhappy house; when all is hush and quiet around him, and all things awe him into solemn gravity; then he stands still, awakes from his dream, grows attentive to himself, discovers the emptiness of his heart, and the treachery of absconded fortune. And what is more natural than for him to enter upon these or similar considerations? what is it then properly that is so much altered within me, or of me, or about me? Is it myself, or my externals? do they essentially belong to me, or did they only stand in a certain affinity with me for a period of time? does my whole,

whole, does my principal happiness consist indeed in them? is the loss of them utterly irreparable? the riches I possessed, were they myself? were the honours and the magnificence that surrounded me, were they me? my ruined health, was that myself? am I not just what I was yesterday and the day before? just as sensible, or just as senseless, just as good, or just as bad, as heretofore? and what is, now, the purport of my existence? Am I here that I may be rich and great, that I may shine and glitter among my brethren, that I may gratify all my sensual desires, that I may fare sumptuously and live joyously every day? That does not depend upon me, that is subject to a thousand accidents! that neither can all men be and do! that neither can any be and do so long as they could wish! and would providence have permitted all these things to be liable to so many revolutions and changes, if they were our sovereign good, if we were to

execute

execute the design of our being by the possession and enjoyment of them? No; that, whatever it be, must be attainable in every station; it must be within the reach of the poor as well as the rich, of the low as well as the high, of the sick as well as the healthy, of the unfortunate as well as the prosperous; it must therefore consist in essential and lasting things. And must not wisdom and virtue, must not spiritual perfection, be this sovereign good? They are internal, and inseparably connected with myself, with me. Of them no misfortune can deprive me! They do not necessarily adhere either to riches or to poverty, either to inferior or to superior station, either to health or sickness! These I may possess, enjoy, and infinitely increase, in the greatest obscurity as well as in the blaze of a court, in a cottage as well as in a palace, in solitude as well as in the most numerous and brilliant assemblies! They can render me serene, contented, and happy, in every condition!

condition! Even death itself cannot deprive me of them! I take them with me into the grave and into the future world! And can I then purchase them at too dear a rate? can that be detrimental to me, can that be a misfortune which makes me a sharer in those goods, or which allows me to enjoy them more, and to a larger extent?—But when tribulations rouze and conduct a man to such reflections, to such considerations, to such conclusions, what a value must they be of to him!

Sufferings and tribulations teach us, farther, to prize more justly the goods of the earth, to compose our desires, and moderate our love of them. How many a person, whose whole heart was wrapped up in these goods, who was the slave of them, who knew no happiness but what they procured or promised him, has learnt in this school to esteem them as what they actually are! When, confined to the bed of of sickness and tormented with pain, he can no longer enjoy them; when trouble and anxiety render them tasteless and insipid; when he suffers under the loss of them; when a change of circumstances has shaken the proud edifice of his fortune, and threatens him with its fall; when death has deprived him of his patron or his friend; then the scales fall off from his eyes; he then intimately feels how much these goods were transitory and worthless, how incapable they are to render a man wholly and constantly happy, and how inadequate to the vehement endeavours that are made to procure them. Now the bonds that bound him are unloosed. Now he trusts no longer to the support of a fragile reed, as though he leaned against a rock. Now he depends no more upon goods that were only lent him, as if they were his unalienable property; confides no more in distinctions that every accident may annul, in strength that may so sud-

denly

denly be loſt, in men that may die to-day, in a life that is ſo ſhort and uncertain. And, ſince his avidity for happineſs ſtill remains equally keen, equally inſatiable; he therefore directs it towards other goods, that are more durable, and more worthy of his endeavours. Now he learns to prefer internals to externals, wiſdom and virtue before honours and wealth, mental joys before ſenſual pleaſures, the inviſible to the viſible, the Creator to the creature. And how greatly muſt he be the gainer thereby! how much ſeldomer now does he exert his faculties in vain! how much more rarely do his hopes and expectations fail him! how much firmer is his welfare fixt! And muſt not tribulations which have helped him to this ſituation, be of great value to him?

In like manner, ſufferings and tribulations very frequently teach us temperance, ſelf-government, and to diſpenſe with many things.

things. This we are forced to of necessity. We cannot, we need not any longer do certain things, any longer lead a certain kind of life, any longer partake of certain amusements. We have lost the means and the pretensions thereto. We must now submit to certain restrictions. By degrees we become used to them; they grow easy, agreeable to us; we find many considerable advantages in them. Now we act from inclination, from principle; we now feel ourselves more free, more independent on outward things; find ourselves less affected by the inconstancy, and less liable to the strokes of fortune; learn to endure quiet, to esteem privacy, to love and profit by retirement, and by all these things become better and completer. What numbers have for the first time learnt to govern themselves, and to understand and enjoy true freedom, in these schools of tribulation! What numbers have been snatched, indeed against their will, but to their real

hap-

happiness, from a round of deceitful dissipations and diversions, where they could not be right-minded, could not enjoy their lives in perfect consciousness, nor be chearful like rational beings, where they were the lamentable sport of their own passions and the passions of others! How many have there been taught to subdue those desires they were formerly forced slavishly to serve, and to deprive themselves of a thousand things, and to forego them without uneasiness, which they held till now to be urgent wants! They are now, in several respects, more circumscribed, but on the whole, more free; are more resigned, but more satisfied with themselves, and happier in their own enjoyment.

Sufferings and tribulations are, fourthly, very often a school of humanity, and the milder virtues of social life; and what a value must this also confer upon them! But too frequently does uninterrupted succefs render us obdurate, infenfible, and unfeeling, to the neceffities of others. The profperous man can feldom form to himfelf a juft reprefentation of the miferies of the diftreffed; his ftation, his affairs, his companies, keep him commonly far away from the fight of them. The healthy and robuft very frequently imagine the complaints of pain and difeafes to be exaggerated or affected, have had no fimilar fenfations, and, if they do not abfolutely difpute thofe of others, yet their ftrong nervous fyftem is but little moved. He with whom all things fucceed, is but too apt to blame another, who laments over defeated plans, over thwarted expectations, over fruftrated labours and endeavours, and to charge him with imprudence and bad management; and how much muft this weaken his compaffion!—But the man that has fuffered himfelf; O Sirs! he feels the forrows of his brother in a different way; he fmarts at the very fight of the fufferer

of

of pain, he mingles his tears with the tears of the mourner, he feels every stroke that falls on another, as if he was smitten himself. Every scar his past sufferings has left upon his heart pains him afresh, and gives him a suggestion of the sufferings of another, that will not allow him to be indifferent or inactive. He who has himself borne the burden of misfortune, feels also how hard it presses when he hears another groan beneath it, and finds within him the strongest impulse to alleviate that burden, if he cannot totally remove it. He who has himself experienced how easily the most prudent projects may be frustrated, how often the best undertakings fail, how often swiftness will not succeed in the race, nor strength in the conflict, nor prudence in business, how much in all these respects depends on fortune and favourable circumstances, he will certainly deem otherwise of him who actually suffers under these experiences, will judge him with much more lenity,

lenity, not condemn him with severity, not impute his misfortune to him as a crime, and not shut up his heart to compassion for him. He who has himself experienced how sweet the participations, the comfort, the assistances of a friend are in sufferings; how they relieve the heart, clear up the prospect, and inspire with fresh hopes, when a man pours out his sorrows into the bosom of another, when he feels that he is not abandoned by all men, that he is not left to suffer alone, and may venture to assure himself of a guide and support even along the ruggedest path of life; oh how will he run to open his heart to the sufferings of his friend and his brother, to give him a vent for his sorrows, to receive his complaints, and to dry up his tears! how eager will the man who has experienced this be to do all that in him lies to throw some light upon his darkness, and to console and revive him! And how gentle, how complacent, how serviceable, how humane,

mane, how beneficent, muſt theſe experiences and ſenſations render him in general
to all mankind!

Sufferings and tribulations are often a
ſchool of many other virtues, and particularly of the ſincereſt devotion. How can we
better learn reſignation, abſolute, unlimited
ſubmiſſion to the will of God, than when
his will is in oppoſition to our own, and
he demands of us the ſacrifice of ſuch things
as had the whole attachment of our heart;
and yet we ſubmit to his will, and acknowledge his will to be right, and good,
and unblamable; and yet without heſita-
tion to make him theſe ſacrifices, let them
be never ſo dear to us, and ſay to him in
ſentiments of the moſt perfect ſincerity;
" Father, not as I will, but as thou wilt—
" Father, thy will be done!" How can
we more ſtrongly teſtify our confidence in
his ſovereign wiſdom and goodneſs, how
ſhew our filial and full compliance with all
his arrangements and diſpenſations, how

our

our conviction that his thoughts and ways are far, far exalted above our thoughts and ways, and are infinitely better and more perfect than ours; than when, even in the midst of misfortunes, we adore him as the all-wise and the all-bountiful, accept without reluctance whatever he ordains, or permits, or does, and compose ourselves by reflections on his superintendency, that he has nothing but perfection and felicity in view, and that his purposes can never fail! How can we exercise ourselves more in faith towards the Almighty, than when we hold it fast and do not let it go, even when reduced to the depth of distress, and even then believe and hope, though we do not see, though all about us is darkness and gloom, when we seem to be forsaken by all, and every thing threatens us with perdition and ruin? And if we are thus exercised and strengthened, by sufferings and tribulations, in resignation to the will of God, in confidence in him,

him, in satisfaction with his ways; if, by their means, we learn the hardest, but at the same time the noblest kind of obedience, the rarest but the purest devotion; must not this evidently promote our advantage and perfection? Must it not bring us nearer to the divinity, and render us more fit for his complacency and the tokens of his favour? Must it not prepare us for an ample recompence in a better world? And must not this give a great value to every affliction and every tribulation?

Yet more. How important, how dear, must sufferings and tribulations render the doctrines and comforts of religion to a man! Religion, to which he formerly perhaps paid but little regard, probably restricted it to certain opinions, or ceremonies and practices, which he but too often thought he could very well dispense with, or which only presented itself to him under a sad and uninviting form, and
                                        which

which he never understood as the friend, the guide, and the comforter, of the human race! When we labour under sufferings, what is more natural than to look out for help? And how seldom with any certitude can we expect it from men! How much seldomer do we actually obtain it from that quarter! and to whom then shall we apply for it but to him who alone can constantly and certainly afford assistance, and does most readily grant it? Yes, Lord, when tribulation cometh, then does a man turn himself to thee! Then does the sentiment of an Almighty, an all-wise, an all-gracious ruler of the world, a father in heaven, which had probably long lain dormant in the soul, again revive; then the inclinations and desires once more take their natural turn; they turn to their creator and preserver, to the eternal source of being and benignity, to him in whom we live, and move, and are! Now has the troubled spirit, the soul toned tossed about upon a sea of sorrows, once more found a harbour of rest, from whence she proceeded, and to which she was destined to return. How differently does she now feel her dependance on the sovereign being, and the intimate and blessed affinity that subsists between the creature and the Creator! She is now no more forsaken, no longer forcibly torn and severed from her former connections, no more a solitary existence in the land of the living! She has how the Lord alway before her, and knows and fees that she walks in his fight, and is protected by his arm, that she lives in his kingdom, is one of his children and subjects, and is concatenated in the most various and intimate manner with the visible and the invisible, the material and the spititual world, by him who comprehends and unites all things in himself. In what an altered light must she now view the doctrine of an all-directing Providence and the government of the Most High! What comfort

comfort muſt ſhe be inſpired with, which ſhe never taſted before! She now no longer appears to be the ſport of chance and the creature of fortune; no more complains in ſullen murmurs of the injuſtice ſhe has undergone; is no longer tormented by rage and rancour againſt the proximate cauſes of her ſufferings; no longer racked by planning and deviſing means of requiting evil with evil. No; it is the Lord's doing; all things are under his ſupreme controul; he diſtributes both proſperous and adverſe fortune, riches and poverty, health and ſickneſs, life and death, according to his good pleaſure, amongſt the children of men; he elevates and he depreſſes, he wounds and heals, conducts to the grave and out of it again, and what he ordains and does muſt neceſſarily be right and good, muſt, ſooner or later, in this way or in that, turn to my advantage, and to the advantage of his whole family on earth! And this, Sirs, this tranquillizes! This
pours

pours balm into the wounded heart! This gives all our sufferings a quite different, a much less terrible aspect!

And how important, how precious must the doctrine of our immortality, of the future and better life, be to the sufferer! When he so acutely feels the emptiness and insufficiency of the present, with all its goods, and advantages, and joys; when so many ties that bound him to it are dissolved or slackened; when the part of his course that still lies before him is lost in obscurity and darkness; when he meets with so many stumbling-blocks, so many impediments and difficulties in it; how comfortable must be the prospect into a superior and a better life! As animating, as when the weary, fainting, persecuted traveller, descries from afar the term of his pilgrimage, the spires of his native land. And with how much greater ease, with how much greater fortitude, will he now
bear

bear the hardſhips of life! How much more ſtrenuouſly and chearfully will he now purſue his courſe, when he runs, not as uncertainly, but expects at the end of it the richeſt recompence for all, the glorious reward of his faith and perſeverance! Oh what a value muſt religion hence acquire in his ſight! and what a value muſt ſufferings and tribulations have, which diſcovered to him the excellency of it, and cauſed him to apply to its comforts!

Sufferings and tribulations are, laſtly, often the moſt efficacious means of improving mankind in general, of rouzing them to a total change in their minds and manners. What all the arguments of reaſon and religion, what all the bounties of God, what all the remonſtrances, exhortations, and intreaties of teachers and friends, what neither the ſtill, ſmall voice of conſcience, nor its loudeſt alarms and reproaches could ever effect; has often been done by ſufferings

ferings and tribulations. All those not unfrequently fall upon the heart of the thoughtless and hardened offender, like water against the smooth surface of a rock, and leave no trace behind. These terrify and stop the inconsiderate wretch that is running headlong to ruin; they forcibly and suddenly arrest him in his wicked course; they strike more deeply into the recesses of his heart; they withdraw, obscure, and dissipate, like dust before the wind, all the shadowy images of happiness that swam about his mind in airy dreams, and will permit him no longer to doubt that he is not what he took himself for, that he has not what he thought he had, that he is unhappy and wretched. His seducers forsake him, or laugh at his distress; his flatterers are silent, and take themselves away; the snares that surround him stand exposed to his view; the precipice he was approaching strikes him dumb with amazement. He stands petrified with horror; he turns his eyes inward;

he muſt bethink himſelf, muſt retreat, muſt ſeek other comforts, other pleaſures, other friends, muſt find out ſome other way to happineſs. No longer dazzled and deceived by outward things, he is and ſees himſelf full of defects and infirmities, ſees himſelf all diſorder and confuſion. And now, when reduced to this condition, with ſuch experiences and ſentiments, he hears the voice of religion, her calls to amendment ſtrike upon his mind, encouragement and inſtruction enter; when the good providence of God ſupplies him with ſome peculiar aſſiſtance, commiſſions to him ſome meſſenger of peace, ſends to him ſome hearty and honeſt friend; how much more diſpoſed muſt he be to liſten to that voice, to follow that call, and to employ theſe means to his amendment!—I will not, however, pretend, that ſufferings and tribulations do always, that they very often, produce ſuch effects in vicious men. They frequently contract, frequently harden,

fre-

frequently pervert them still more. Yet many have got the rudiments of reflection and amendment in this school. Many have here first received the incitement, many have embraced the first resolves, have made the first steps of their return to the path of duty and virtue. Many have been thankful to heaven for having been humbled by sufferings.

Thus chastening is productive of salutary effects in them that are exercised thereby, by rendering them virtuous and good. Thus, therefore, sufferings and tribulations are of real and often of very great value. Thus are they the benefactions of Providence, and sources of happiness. If storms and tempests in the physical world drive destructive diseases away from our dwellings, and bring life, and health, and fertility with them; so likewise may the blasts of misfortune in the moral world rouze the supine from their dangerous slumber, drive away mifts and vapours from the eyes, and awaken the torpid to new powers and action, fharpen the dull feelings of the palfied finner, and reftore to life the fpiritually dead. Far be it then from us to let fufferings and tribulations flacken our confidence in the unalterable and never-failing goodnefs of our Father in heaven! No; even they are effects and demonftrations of it. No; with filial reverence will we accept the cup of forrow from his parental hand, and never doubt, even whilft drinking out its bitter dregs, that it is wholefome medicine, by which he reftores us to health and life.

ESTIMATE XXXIV.

THE VALUE OF A GOOD REPUTATION.

A good name is rather to be chosen than great riches, and loving favour rather than silver or gold.   Proverbs xxii. 1.

ESTIMATE

OF THE

VALUE

of

A GOOD REPUTATION

A good name is rather to be chosen than great riches, and loving favour rather than silver or gold.
            Proverb. xxii. 1.

THE VALUE OF A GOOD REPUTATION.

VERY often it happens that a man is negligent and careless about matters of great importance, only becauſe he does not know their value, or does not ſufficiently attend to it; or, becauſe he does not think the privation of them to be ſo prejudicial and irreparable as it really is. This is but too frequently the caſe in regard to the time allotted to us to paſs upon earth. It is not believed or conſidered to be deſtined to affairs, on the ſucceſsful tranſacting whereof,

whereof, not only our welfare in this world depends, but likewise our contingencies in that which is to come. It is not believed or considered, that this precious time is very liable to be lost, that lost time can never be recalled, and that the benefits which we suffer to escape us by the waste or the abuse of it can be compensated by nothing. It is not believed or considered, that each day, each hour of life, when regarded in its connection with futurity, is of the utmost importance, that it may frequently be decisive. Hence it is that most men are so prodigal of their time; hence so great a part of it is trifled away either in doing nothing, or in childish amusements; hence it is that concerns of the greatest consequence are so much neglected; hence it is that one day is suffered to pass after another, one month after another, one year after another, before a man seriously sets about his improvement and his salvation.

Just

Juſt as we do with our time, ſo do we not unfrequently with the good name of our neighbour. It does not always happen, it happens indeed but rarely, that we ſay and do ſuch things as are prejudicial to our neighbour's fame from wickedneſs and a deſire to hurt. But it is not ſufficiently believed or conſidered that ſo much depends upon it; that it is ſo eaſily injured or loſt, and that this damage can ſo ſeldom be repaired or made good. It is not believed or conſidered, that thereby not only the well-being and comfort of the private peſons againſt whom the offence is committed are diſturbed, but even the good of the whole ſociety is injured by various ways. Hence it is, that a man ſo often gives full licence to his tongue in judging of his neighbour; ſo often ſacrifices truth to wit, and chriſtian affection and forbearance to the deſire of pleaſing; ſo often utters harmful or ambiguous expreſſions of others, without being fully perſuaded

that

that they are well-founded, or making himself the flighteft reproaches thereon. This being the cafe, there can be no better means of attacking this failing, and of rendering us more circumfpect on this matter, than by reprefenting it in its real complexion, and thus exciting in our minds a lively fentiment of its importance. This is what I now purpofe to attempt.

I will fhew you the great value of a good reputation, and remind you of the duties we owe in this refpect to ourfelves and to our neighbour.

By the reputation or good name of a man, I underftand the general confideration wherein he ftands with all thofe that know him perfonally or by the report of others; and this confideration is grounded on the good opinion the public has of his underftanding, of his integrity, of his way of thinking and behaving, of his fkill in
certain

certain bufineffes, arts, and fciences, or is fupported by other advantages and merits attributed to him. On this good character, I fay, extremely much depends; it is of very great value; for by it we are rendered much happier, much more generally ufeful, and not unfrequently morally better, than we fhould or could be without it.

Our good name, in the firft place, promotes our happinefs, fo far as our welfare is dependent on it. To this happinefs thoufands of perfons muft contribute out of what they have. It is a large and fpacious edifice, that we indeed raife ourfelves, to which we lay at leaft the foundation, and muft conftantly labour in carrying on the fuperftructure. But this we can never do effectually without the concurrence of others; we can never bring it to any confiderable degree of perfection, without them, nor properly maintain it when finifhed. One while we are in want of the

plans

plans and advice, then of the greater abilities and force, now of the assistance and support, or encouragement of our fellow-beings, for effecting our designs, for successfully prosecuting our affairs and undertakings, for quietly enjoying our possessions and profits, or for consoling us under adverse events.

But shall our fellow-creatures serve us with their plans and advice? shall they employ their abilities and force to our benefit? shall they assist, support, and encourage us? Then must they have a stronger incitement thereto than mere self-interest can give them. These advantages are not always; they are but seldom; and some of them can never be purchased. They are the fruit of the esteem and the benevolence with which our brethren are affected towards us; and this esteem, this benevolence, is founded on the good opinion they entertain of us. In proportion as this good opinion

opinion is oppofed and enfeebled, fufpicion or difefteem take place; and in the. fame proportion alfo will their readinefs and ardour to promote our happinefs be diminifhed, and their benevolence and obliging behaviour towards us will change into coldnefs and indifference.———Only put the queftion to yourfelves: why do you fo readily, why is it fo agreeable to you to afford all poffible fervice to certain perfons; and why do you find it fo unpleafant, why are you forced to ufe fo much conftraint and felf denial, to do for others any thing beyond what the ftricteft juftice requires of you? Does it not principally proceed from this, that you have a good opinion of the former, and a bad opinion of the latter; that you efteem the one fort, and defpife the other? How readily does a man communicate his intelligence and his beft advice to him whom he accounts a fenfible and an honeft man, that knows how to efteem and to ufe good counfel! How chear-

chearfully does a man impart of his confequence or his means to the perfon on whofe fincerity and uprightnefs he can fafely depend! How willingly do we afford help and fupport to him whom we believe to have no other than honeft intentions and upright views, and would be ready, in fimilar cafes, to afford the fame help and fupport to us! How heartily does a man confide in him whofe misfortunes cannot be imputed to his own faulty conduct, but to unavoidable and unaccountable events, and whom he could fincerely wifh to have been fuccefsful, for the fake of his good qualities and deferts! On the other hand, who would offer advice to the fool, or open himfelf to the artful? who would truft his means or his countenance to the deceiver? who would readily afford help and fupport to the bafe or the ungrateful? who would endeavour to comfort the wilful tranfgreffor? Certainly then a great part of our happinefs, or of our outward welfare,

depends

depends on the behaviour of our fellow-creatures towards us; certainly likewife their behaviour towards us is determined by the good or the bad reputation we have in their account.

This is not all. We are defigned for focial life, for intercourfe with other men, for the participation of our mutual joys and pleafures. Apart from all our rational fellow-creatures, fecluded from their focieties and pleafures, left alone to ourfelves and our folitary reflections and feelings, we could either not be happy at all, or not in fo high a degree. The genial fentiment of benevolence and friendfhip, that pure and abundant fource of pleafure, would foon be extinct, for want of a fupply; and the oppofite fenfations of fpleen, vexation, and mifanthropy, would fucceed in its room. But if focial life is to have any charms for us; if intercourfe with others is to be agreeable,

able, if they are to take part in what befalls us, and to admit us to a share in their joys and their pleasures; then must we stand in good repute amongst them. They must ascribe to us such qualities or dispositions as are of some value in their eyes, and render us not unworthy of their friendship and converse. At least, they must not charge us with any thing, they must not believe us to be capable of any thing, that merits contempt or abhorrence.

A natural and unconstrained behaviour, a free and easy communication of our sentiments and feelings, a frank but not injurious opinion of what we see and hear, of what is said and done; a mutually earnest, but not a studied and troublesome endeavour to be agreeable; are undoubtedly the real delights of social life, the greatest charms of friendly intercourse. But can these subsist where the members of society are not connected by mutal esteem? Will any

any one, who, whether by his own fault or not, stands in bad repute among the rest, be admitted to the enjoyment of these satisfactions? Will not people shun the conversation of one that lies under the imputation of a weak understanding or a wicked heart, who is reckoned a hypocrite, or a slanderer, or a severe and ludicrous censor, or a sower of dissention, or to whose charge any other bad dispositions or actions are laid? And if one cannot absolutely avoid his company on account of our circumstances and situation, can it be imagined that we shall take much pains to promote his pleasure? will people do justice to his character, his judgements, and his conduct? will people shew themselves to him in their natural colours, and by that means furnish him with opportunity and encouragement to do so too? will they not rather interpret his most indifferent gestures, his most harmless words and actions, nay his most insignificant looks, by the prepoffeffions they have imbibed against him? will not his acquaintance be either utterly cold and reserved towards him, or, by a forced regard and friendship, rather confound than comfort him? Certainly, let a man have what eminent capacities and endowments of mind, what good qualities, what great merits soever; but let Malice or Levity spread injurious reports about him, reports which possess a certain degree of credibility; and he will soon be deprived of the best part of the social satisfactions and pleasures which his talents, his qualities, his deserts, gave him great right to expect; he will probably soon be reduced to live entirely alone, or at least to confine his conversation to the persons dependent upon him; and how much must this impair his happiness, how many sources of it must it exclude him from enjoying! While to him, on the other hand, who is in possession of a good reputation, all these sources of pleasure and joy stand open;

open; and he may even with far less talents and merits, with far greater failings and infirmities, than the other has, receive from them various kinds of satisfaction and happiness.

But, as a good reputation contributes much to our happiness, inasmuch as our outward welfare and our intercourse with others depend upon it, so shall we thereby become more generally useful than we otherwise could, and may contribute much more to the happiness of others, than we could do without it; and this in various ways.

For being useful to society, it is not enough that we possess certain capacities and skill in many respects; that we are masters of certain arts or sciences, or certain kinds of trade and commerce; that we execute with industry and punctuality the concerns intrusted to us; but others must likewise believe and know that we have these capacities and aptitudes, that we understand these matters, and that we may safely be trusted with them. And, as generally speaking we are not the only persons who can render these or other services to society, then mankind must be induced to accept them at our hands; and to this end they must ascribe to us such qualities and distinctive merits by which we may attract their regard and conciliate their esteem. At least, we must have no base or doubtful character in the eye of the publick, and our conduct must be irreproachable, if our services are to be preferred to those of others. We must therefore have a good name among our fellow-creatures; they must have a good opinion of us.

Of what service, in this respect, is wisdom to the wise, to the scholar his learning, to the patriot his vigilant and generous

nerous ardour for the common welfare, if men will not elect them to such offices, and place them in such stations, as may enable them to shew their wisdom, their learning, their patriotic dispositions, and apply them to purposes of importance? But will men ordinarily confer these offices and posts upon them, if they entertain a mean opinion of them; if they take the wise man for an obstinate and fantastical fellow, the scholar for a cross-grained, upstart pedant, the patriot for a self-interested and ambitious pretender? or though they should indeed allow their eminent qualities, yet at the same time should charge them with such blemishes in their character, as should take away all their lustre?

The case is exactly the same with the artist, with the artificer, with the merchant, with the lawyer, and others. Shall the artist or the artificer exert himself in his art or profession; shall he bring himself to a certain degree of perfection therein, and so render himself truly useful to society; then must he have much work of art or industry to execute; and this will not be given him, if they who are to employ him have not a good opinion of his talents or his skill, or a regard for him on account of his personal or moral qualities. Shall the merchant pursue his affairs with success; shall he, by a diffusive and profitable commerce, promote the welfare of his countrymen, and of society in general; then must he be taken, both at home and abroad, for an intelligent, penetrating, active, and upright man; he must be thought to understand his business well, and to transact it with carefulness and caution; and in the degree that this belief is weakened or diminished, to the same degree will his activity for the general advantage be reduced, and his influence on the whole be lessened. Shall, lastly, the lawyer be really useful by his knowledge

of

of the laws of the land, and of the manner of proceeding in litigations, or even by his eloquence; then muſt he ſtand, with the parties as well as with the bench, in the reputation of a well-informed, acute, and ſolid man, as a friend to truth and juſtice, as a foe to all ſiniſter evaſions, every ſpecies of ſubterfuge and corruption; and the more general and unqueſtioned this reputation is, ſo much the more is he in a capacity, by diſcreet diſſuaſions from perilous ſuits, or by friendly accommodations of controverſies already begun, or by a reſolute proſecution of right, to contribute to the common good. In ſhort, without the help of a good reputation, no man will eaſily find opportunity to afford conſiderable ſervice to human ſociety; and by the loſs of it, all the capacities and means a man may poſſeſs to that end will generally be rendered uſeleſs.

Still more. Though by means of the place we hold, or the office we fill in human society, we have the moſt frequent occaſions of applying our talents to the general welfare; yet we ſhall ſeldom be able to do ſo with ſucceſs, unleſs we bear a good reputation. The purity of our intentions will always be called into doubt; our beſt propoſals will be rejected. Our moſt public-ſpirited endeavours will fail, for want of countenance and ſupport, or will even be attacked by violent and obſtinate oppoſition. We ſhall very frequently exert our abilities and faculties in vain, and always, even by the ſincereſt applications of them, effect comparatively but little. Whereas the better the opinion men have of us, the more confidence will they repoſe in our ſkill and integrity; with ſo much better ſucceſs ſhall we do what we ought in virtue of our office and vocation; ſo much the fewer hindrances and difficulties ſhall we meet with in the execution

execution of our good defigns, or in the profecution of falutary projects. Good men will fupport and animate us in them according to their means; and bad men will not eafily venture to commence hoftilities with us.

Of how great importance, in this refpect, for example, is the good fame of a prince, of a minifter, or a magiftrate! So long as the rulers or the perfons entrufted with the public adminiftration are reputed to be the wife and good fathers of the people, fo long as the publick afcribe eminent abilities and virtues to them, fo long as they are generally thought to be honeft and faithful; fo long will it be eafy for them to govern their fubjects according to their pleafure, to give currency and weight to their laws and ordinances, to accomplifh their aims without oppofition, and to unite, if not all, yet the majority of the members of the ftate, in the profecution

cution of them. But do men once begin to doubt of their abilities, or of their steadiness and integrity, and these doubts become general; do men once charge them with self-interestedness, or tyrannical dispositions, or even indifferency to the common welfare; they will find but little support, even though they are sincerely acting consistently with their duty, and are labouring for the prosperity of the country; but will meet with much opposition. Men will not trust to their most express declarations and assertions; will find fault with their wisest measures; despise and transgress their most salutary laws; murmur at their most reasonable demands; and pay them no other than a forced, and of consequence a very imperfect and defective obedience.

How much, in this respect, depends on the repute wherein a public teacher of religion stands with his audience! Do they doubt

doubt of his integrity; do they think they discover a contradiction between his doctrine and his conduct; does he fall under the reproach of a hireling, who, for the sake of lucre or of an empty honour, maintains what he does not believe, and extols what he does not chuse to perform: then, let his talents be never so eminent, his discourses be never so excellent and melting, his diligence and zeal in discharging the duties of his function be never so great; yet with all this he will accomplish but little; it is likely he will effect not half so much as another that has far meaner talents, discourses not near so elegantly, exerts a far more moderate zeal and industry, who has a reputation for sincerity and an exemplary conduct.

And the case is just the same with us all, in whatever station we are placed. The better the opinion that men have of us, the more easily and effectually may we
be

be useful to others, and promote the general welfare; so much the readier acceptation will our advice obtain; so much the deeper impression will our exhortations, admonitions, and corrections, make; so much the greater influence will our good example have. Let the man who has once lost his good name, who, for instance, has once been pronounced a bigot or a hypocrite, let him perform never such generous actions; let him never so feelingly exhort to virtue and piety; let him exhibit never so much devotion, or meekness, or moderation, in his words and deeds, whom will all this move? whom will it allure to imitation? On the other hand, who does not account it his glory to follow him whom he himself esteems, and on whom a favourable judgement is passed by the whole community? So very much depends the success of our endeavours, of the best use of our capacities and powers, and the ability of doing as much good in the world

as

as we might, on the good or bad repute wherein we stand!

Hence, in fine, it arises, that a good reputation may even contribute much to our moral improvement and perfection; and that, on the contrary, the loss of it often misguides a man into the grossest profligacy, into a completely immoral and dissolute conduct. This is a matter that deserves the utmost attention, and sets the great value of a good reputation beyond all manner of doubt. If we know that we are generally allowed to possess certain aptitudes, good qualities, and virtues; that we are held incapable of any unjust, or base, or sinister actions; that much good is said of our understanding and our heart; that we are acknowledged to be upright and estimable members of society; what a strong incitement must it be to exert these abilities and good qualities; actually to exhibit these virtues; carefully to avoid
these

these bad actions; to do honour to our understanding and our heart; and to preserve the estimation wherein we stand by an inoffensive and a praise-worthy conduct!

I am not ignorant, that he who is incited to goodness, and refrains from what is wrong, from these considerations alone, does not yet deserve the name of a virtuous man; we neither can, however, nor ought we to be indifferent to the judgement of our fellow-creatures; and when the concern for the preservation of our good name is accompanied and supported by some more noble motives, it may very lawfully be a means of facilitating us in the discharge of our duties, and so, by rendering us more attentive to all our discourses and actions, promote our perfection. At least, the wrong is left undone, and the good is done; and the more frequently, even in views that are not of the very first quality, we omit the one and do the other, so much in
pro-

proportion muft our difpofition to the one be weakened, and our aptitude to the other be increafed, and fo much the more eafily fhall we be acted upon by the nobler incitements to integrity and virtue.

On the other hand, is the good name loft; then, with moft men, that is loft which to them was the ftrongeft prefervative from follies and fins. They had before abftained from many obliquities of conduct to which they had fufficient inclination and appetite, for the fake of preferving the character of honeft men, or of being refpected by others; they probably have done violence to themfelves; have performed many a juft, reafonable, beneficent, generous action, in direct oppofition to their own principles and propenfities; have probably, at different times, made a furrender of their private advantage to the public benefit, for the pleafure arifing from fame; they have, at leaft, avoided every
thing

thing that might be offenfive to others and excite indignation. At prefent they find they have miffed of their aim, fince mankind refufe them what they had a right to pretend to as a compenfation for the violence they did to themfelves; fince they are now judged and treated as if they had done juft the reverfe; they now no longer keep any meafures, but wholly abandon themfelves to their propenfities and paffions. They at once give up all hope of maintaining the reputation of honeft, worthy men, and ufeful citizens; concern themfelves no more therefore about their fame; defpife the cenfures of their fellow-beings; and never inquire any more whether an action be offenfive or inoffenfive, laudable or fcandalous; and thus, by conftantly making farther advances in follies and diforders, they are ever becoming more averfe to all good, and more incapable of it, till at length they fink into a ftate of infenfibility

bility and hardness of heart, that renders their amendment nearly impossible.

And now what conclusion are we to draw from all this? How shall we frame our behaviour according to this truth, which we cannot deny? It imposes a variety of important duties upon us; and I will wind up this discussion with a few words of exhortation to the observance of them.

Is a good reputation of so great a value? Does it contribute so much to the promotion of our welfare and pleasures? Without it, can we, even with the best intentions, neither duly exercise our gifts and abilities, nor be really useful to human society? Oh, strive then to your utmost to preserve this precious jewel, you that are in possession of it! Set a watch, in this respect, over all your words and actions, and sedulously avoid every thing that may weaken the good opinion you hold in the minds of men. Do not imagine that this concern is unbecoming a virtuous and noble-spirited man. It will be unbecoming if the desire of pleasing be the great motive of your actions; if you only regulate your behaviour, without regard to the rules of justice and equity, by the judgement of other men; or if you prize their esteem and their applause more than the favour and applause of your God.

No; our first question must ever be, What is right? What is good? What is consistent with my nature and the will of God? What is my obligation as a man, as a christian, as a citizen, as a father of a family? And, in determining these questions, neither the approbation nor the censure of men must be of any account whatever. We must act by certain principles, and to these we must ever adhere. By this means, however, we shall infallibly secure

cure to ourselves the esteem of the best and worthiest part of the community, and, in the generality of occasions, may rely on their approbation, without anxiously seeking it, or making it our principal aim.

But, is an action to be done that falls under no particular law, that we may either perform or neglect, wherein we may proceed in this manner or in that; in that case we direct our conduct so as best to conduce to the confirming of our good reputation. By so doing, we not only are not chargeable with any criminal passion of fame; we act not only with prudence, but in perfect consistence with our duty, which enjoins us to do every thing by which we may mediately become useful to others, or acquire a greater and surer influence on the advancement of the general good. A good name may be weakened and lost not only by the actual commission of evil, but even by the appearance

ance of it; not only by unjuft and mean, but even by innocent and imprudent difcourfes and actions. Abftain then from all appearances of evil, and walk with circumfpection and prudence.

If, farther, a good reputation be fo highly valuable, then imprint it deeply on your mind, that you cannot attack the good name of your neighbour, or bring it by any means into contempt, without caufing great harm to the whole fociety, and rendering yourfelf guilty of the moft crying injuftice, and frequently of the uttermoft degree of inhuman cruelty. Rather rob your neighbour of his goods; wound him in his perfon; plunge him into poverty and indigence! You will generally hurt him lefs, and do him a more fupportable injury, than by unrighteoufly depriving him of the efteem he poffeffes amongft his fellow-beings. By this efteem he may repair the other wrongs you do him;
with-

without it, as it frequently happens, neither opulence, nor station, nor life itself, have any charms for him. Regard not, therefore, the reputation of your brother, be his condition in life what it may, as a matter of sport, as a subject for merriment, on which we may boldly display our wit. Constantly reflect how easily the good name of the inoffensive may be injured, and how difficult it is to heal the wounds we give it. An ambiguous word, a mysterious look, an eloquent silence, a sneering smile, a malicious BUT, is more than sufficient to make the most unfavourable impression of the character or the conduct of a person on the unthinking, the credulous, or the malicious hearer, to occasion the most disadvantageous reports, or to undermine the credit of a harmless or deserving member of society. Unhappily such a report may so quickly spread, the raised suspicion may so rapidly gain confirmation, it may collect so many circumstances together which render

render it credible, that it is often immediately no more in your power to repair the injuſtice you have done. In vain would you now recall your imprudent expreſſions; in vain attempt to ſlur over the matter as a miſunderſtanding, an inadvertent eſcape, a jeſt, or an ingnificant ſportive conceit; in vain will you even implore forgiveneſs of the injured man! Probably the alteration of your language or your behaviour will be attributed to fear, or to complaiſance, or to ſelf-love, or to certain confederacies and combinations ſince made; it will be long ere you can effect a perſuaſion that there was nothing at all in the matter, and probably it may require whole years before you can, even by the moſt earneſt endeavours, be able to efface the impreſſion you have made upon others to the prejudice of your neighbour. And if, with all your pains, you are unable to do this; then have you, probably for ever, deſtroyed the peace of an innocent man;

ſapped

sapped the foundation of his happiness and of those that belong to him; rendered a useful member of civil society unprofitable or of little service; you have probably deprived him of all heart to amendment had he been so inclined; and him, whom a concern for his good name retained within the bounds of moderation and honour, you have rendered alike indifferent both to honour and to shame. What a flagrant enormity! How dreadful will it be to you in the hour of serious reflection, or on your bed of death! Can we then ever be too circumspect, too conscientious, when we have to do with our neighbour's fame? Surely no; the greater the value, and the more irreparable the loss of it, so much the more sacred must it be to us; and so much the more must we abstain from every thing that may lessen or impair it. Let us then bridle our tongue and keep a watch at the door of our lips, and banish from our heart all envy, all hatred, all bitterness, and animosity against our brethren. Let us abhor and detest not only manifest lying and slandering, but likewise regard and avoid all base defamation, all hard and severe judgements on our neighbour, as sins which can by no means be made to consist with the philanthropy and the character of a real christian. Let us put on the bowels of compassion, friendliness, meekness, gentleness, and patience, as becomes the children of God, and the disciples of Jesus; bearing and forgiving one another with the most cordial affection; and so act with all men, and so judge of every one, as we should desire, in similar circumstances, that they would act by us and judge of our behaviour. But, above all things, let us clothe ourselves with love, which is the bond of all perfection.

ESTIMATE XXXV.

OF CONVERSION FROM A BAD COURSE of LIFE.

I will arise, and go to my father, and will say unto him, Father, I have sinned against heaven, and before thee, and am no more worthy to be called thy son: make me as one of thy hired servants.
Luke xv. 18. 19.

BATH:

A

POEM.

VERSES

FROM

OCTAVO,

OF CONVERSION FROM A BAD COURSE OF LIFE.

A Person that awakes, from the carelessness and negligence into which he has been lulled by vice, to remorse and conversion, is beautifully depicted in the Gospel under the image of the Prodigal Son. He first becomes sensible of his misery. Till now he thought himself happy in having shaken off the authority and withdrawn himself from the vigilance of his father. The unbounded freedom he enjoyed, the extravagant and dissolute life he he had led, the tumultuous pleasures he met with on all hands, flattered his desires. They beguiled his soul; they concealed futurity from his view; and he thought he had no reason to repent of his senseless choice. But having shortly run through all his means, sunk into the extremities of poverty and contempt, must put up with the vilest servitude, and the slenderest provision, and with all can scarcely support his life; he wakes from his wretched delusion. The visionary representations of pleasure and happiness by which he has been hitherto deceived, are now vanished away. He finds himself cheated in his expectations. He can no longer conceal his wretchedness from himself. He severely feels the deplorable consequences of his foolish conduct; he groans under the burden of it; and these painful sensations compel him to think seriously on freeing himself from them.

Juſt ſo it is with the man that awakes from the lethargy of vice. He proceeds for a long time ſecure and careleſs in his wicked ways, breaks every tie of religion and virtue, refuſes due obedience to his Creator and Lord, and takes that for freedom which is in fact the hardeſt and moſt ſhameful bondage. The ſinful deſires which he blindly follows, captivate him with their deceitful charms; they promiſe him complete pleaſures and joy; and he fondly imagines he has found out the way that leads to true felicity. The violent calls of his paſſions ſtifle the voice of his reaſon and his conſcience; the affairs and diſſipations of this world guard the entrance to his ſoul againſt all ſedate reflection, and, like a man intoxicated with the flames of drink, ſees not the danger that awaits him. But when the poiſon of ſin has had its effect; when diſquiet, vexation, and diſguſt, take place of pleaſure; when pain and ſickneſs, or other adverſe

verse events, stimulate him, as it were, to reflect on himself and his moral condition; when the loss of his property, the sudden death of his friend, the unexpected failure of his plans, or other striking occurrences fill him with dismay; when the light of truth, in this suspension of the passions, in this silence of the heart, darts upon his spirit, and the darkness of prejudice and error, which had hitherto blinded him, is dispelled; he then begins to understand the deceitfulness of sin, then its fascinating charms are dissipated before him. They appear to him as ghastly and detestable as they really are; and he is seized with the utmost astonishment that he could ever be imposed on by such empty impostures. He now feels the degrading, the cruel shackles by which he is bound, and sees that he, who thought himself erewhile so free, is in fact the most wretched of slaves. He now tastes how bitter the fruits are of sin, and experiences what sorrow and anguish of

heart

heart it occasions when a man forsakes the Lord his God, and esteems any thing but him for his sovereign good. His false repose is now come to an end; his security makes way for trouble and affright; his foolish hopes are all cast down; his conscience goads and condemns him. He now shudders at the danger he before derided with arrogant scorn; he feels the manifold misery he has brought on himself by his sins and the disorder that prevailed in his soul; he confesses that nothing can render him more deplorably wretched than he is; and this confession begets in him an earnest desire to be delivered and happy.

But to make this acknowledgement effective, and these desires wholesome, he must now faithfully follow the light that has dawned upon him. He must carefully cherish the good emotions that have succeeded to his insensiblity, and apply himself to such considerations as may move him

him to firm and unchangeable resolutions. The poor unhappy youth in the parable was sensible not only to his misery, but he compared his forlorn condition with the various and great advantages which he might have enjoyed in the house of his father. " How many hired servants, says he, of my father, have bread enough and to spare, and I perish with hunger !" As he had thoughtlessly rejected them all, he now reflects with the greatest concern on the past, the present, and the future. How happy, thought he, how happy I formerly was, when I lived in my father's house, and under his inspection, when I was cherished by his complacency, and nurtured by his care ! how tender was his affection for me ! how active and unwearied his zeal for promoting my welfare ! what would have been wanting to my happiness, had I but known how to prize and employ my advantages ! how tranquil, how securely, how contentedly, could I have past my days,

days, had I but been prudent! Difmal reflection! How fadly are my circumftances altered! how low am I fallen; the purfuit of imaginary freedom has made me a flave! my contempt for paternal authority has fubjected me to the dominion of a foreign and fevere controul! my difcontentednefs with what I had has brought me to the extremeft diftrefs. And what dreadful profpects lie before me! Soon muft I perifh with hunger. Death approaches me with hafty ftrides; and I perceive him in his moft dreadful form — Yet I ftill live; all hope of deliverance is not yet extinct. I ftill difcern a little efcape before me, by which I may perhaps avoid my ruin. Have I not a father? and is not a father indowed with indulgence and compaffion? Had I not better try all things, than give myfelf up to comfortlefs defpondency, or fink into defpair?

So thought the lost young man; and so the repentant sinner thinks, who is in earnest, and anxious about his salvation. What a blessing, says he to himself, have I voluntarily rejected by my sins and my follies! Happy had it been for me, if I had hearkened to the voice of God and of my conscience, if I had observed their affectionate admonitions and suggestions, if I had kept my innocency, and remained faithful to my duty! How rational, how equitable, how reasonable are all the commands of God! and how happy would the observing of them have made me! The inestimable favour of the Supreme Being, peace of mind, contentment of sprit, the consciousness of my integrity, the esteem and love of all the good, the certain hope of everlasting happiness, would have delighted all my days; they would have sweetened the cup of life, and have alleviated the burden of its cares; they would have shed divine transport upon my soul.

Under the protection of my heavenly Father I should have dwelt in safety; and in the shadow of his wings have had no want or misfortune to fear. And these blessings have I sacrificed to the fallacious pleasures of sin! I have shaken off the mild authority of my Creator and Benefactor, and am now under the cruel sway of the most shameful and the most corrupted desires. All the powers of my spirit are enervated; disorder and contradiction disturb my soul; wickedness is become, as it were, a second nature to me; and I feel myself too weak to enter the lists against it, and recover the freedom I have lost. God has hid his gracious countenance from me. I have brought upon myself his terrible displeasure, and live at a most deplorable distance from him. And what will become of me if death overtake me in this condition, if I am cited to appear in this sad condition before the Judge of the living and the dead? How can I support his look? how can I stand before him! With what excuses can I palliate my premeditated and so often repeated violations of his law, or mitigate my ingratitude and my defection! What a severe but righteous condemnation have I to dread! How horrible will be my portion for eternity! Oh that I had not sinned! Oh that I had never forsaken my Father and my Redeemer! never cast off the fear of heaven! Who will now redeem me from this misery! Where shall I find help and deliverance!—But, continues the contrite sinner, is there then no precious gleam of hope, no ray of comfort, to my amazed soul? no means in reserve for rescuing me from deserved condemnation, for becoming happy yet? Oh, I have read that the Lord is gracious, long-suffering, and plenteous in mercy; that he will not despise the broken and contrite heart; that such as return to him he will in no wise cast out. I have read that Jesus is the Saviour of men; and that all who trust in him,

him, and follow his sacred precepts, shall be received into the kingdom of heaven! Perhaps then he will have compassion on me, and give me grace for justice, if I humble myself before him, and turn to him with all my heart.—No.—My misery is, alas, too great! The danger I am in is too imminent, to allow me room to hope that any thing can snatch me from it.

Such are the agitations and fears of the returning sinner; till, his spirit worn out with woe, his eyes dissolved in tears, and his heart all rent with compunction, he takes up the conclusion of the Prodigal in the parable.

I will arise, says the contrite youth, and go to my father, and will say unto him, "Father, I have sinned against heaven, and before thee, and am no more worthy to be called thy son; make me as one of thy hired servants." I will immediately embrace

embrace the only means still left me to employ, for avoiding utter ruin, before it be too late, and all repentance be in vain. I will exert the little strength I have remaining, to hasten from the abyss that lies open before me. The smallest delay may be fatal to me. To regain my lost contentment shall from this instant be my sole concern; and nothing shall be too hard for me to undertake that can favour my design. Let the shame and confusion be as great as it may, into which the consciousness of my follies and the sight of my injured father will throw me; let the reproaches I have to expect from him be as cutting as they will to my vanity and pride; cost what resolution and self-denial it may at first to renounce my wicked habits, and to satisfy my so long neglected duties; nothing shall prevent me from returning to him whom I have so senselessly forsaken, and asking succour of him who alone is disposed and able to help me. I will go and throw my-

self

self at his feet; and, instead of thinking on evasion or excuse, I will condemn myself, and cast myself entirely on his mercy. It is no austere, no inexorable master; it is a compassionate and tender father with whom I have to do. What has not a son to hope for from such a father? Yes, his own heart will speak pity for me, he will shew mercy towards me; and this shall be my inducement to testify my gratitude to him by a willing and faithful obedience, and to render myself worthy of his favour by a total alteration of my sentiments and my conduct.

The repentant sinner takes up the same resolutions. He trusts not to a deceitful and inefficient sorrow. He is not contented with making bitter lamentations on his wretched condition, or barely wishing to become better, without putting his hand to the work. He wastes not his time in useless doubt or in dangerous hesitation.

My life, says he, is passing quickly away; it may unexpectedly come to an end. Death, judgement, and eternity, are ever advancing towards me; they may seize me at unawares. Shall not I then hasten to deliver my soul? Shall I not work while it is day, ere the night come when no man can work? There is but one way left to avoid perdition. Shall I hesitate one moment about betaking myself to it? Life and death, blessing and cursing, are now before me. Still I have an opportunity of chusing between them. Who can tell whether that will continue to me if I stand longer doubting? Is it difficult for me now to subdue my sinful desires, to quit my bad habits, break with my bad companions, and reform my dissolute life? will it not every day become still harder? Will not my servitude be growing constantly more severe, my propensity to vice more strong, my soul more corrupted, and consequently my amendment still more impracticable?

Shall

Shall I not by thefe means be heaping fin upon fin, and punifhment upon punifhment, and fo at length deprive myfelf of all hope of forgivenefs? No; to-day, that I hear the voice of the Lord, while his grace is yet offered to me, to-day will I follow his affectionate call, and earneftly implore that divine compaffion which alone can make me happy. My refolution is taken, and nothing fhall hinder me from bringing it to effect. I will arife and go to my heavenly Father, from whom I am now at fo great a diftance, whofe favour and protection I have fo madly caft off. I will bow myfelf before his offended majefty, acknowledge my tranfgreffions, and intreat his compaffion with a broken and a contrite heart. I will folemnly renounce all my fins, and devote myfelf to the fervice of God and the practice of virtue. Have I hitherto fhaken off his juft and gentle authority; it fhall now be my greateft delight and glory to pay him an unreferved obedience,

obedience, and to fulfill the duties of a faithful subject in his kingdom. Have I hitherto directed my life by my irregular desires and the corrupted principles of the men of the world; henceforward the law of the Most High shall be the sole and unalterable rule of my manners. Have I hitherto provided only for my person and my earthly condition; henceforward, the care of my soul, and my happiness in the future world, shall be the ultimate aim of all my endeavours. The support which God hath promised to the sincere will be mighty in my weakness. He will assist me in conquering every difficulty; and I trust assuredly that I shall find his yoke to be easy, and his burden light; that I shall experience that his commandments are not grievous.

If the resolutions of the repentant sinner be thus composed; if they be grounded on self-inspection, on consideration and firm con-

conviction; if they be taken with seriousness and sincerity; then will they certainly be brought to effect. The Prodigal Son suffered himself not to be turned aside from his purpose. He immediately began to put them in execution. He arose and came to his father, and said unto him, " Father, I have sinned against heaven and in thy sight, and am no more worthy to be called thy son." I have outrageously offended both God and thee; I have rendered myself utterly unworthy of thy parental love. Thus did he humble himself before his father. He acknowledged his past offences, and sought no subterfuges, no extenuations of his guilt, but confessed them for what they really were. He owned that he had thereby forfeited all pretences to the privileges he had before enjoyed in his father's house. He discovered a sincere remorse at his enormities, and implored his favour and forgiveness. He puts himself anew under his guidance and authority, promises fresh obedience

obedience to all his commands, and returns effectively to his duty. And in this particular confifts the true repentance and converfion which God requires from man. He muft confefs the multitude, the greatnefs, the enormity of his fins; and, inftead of thinking on his juftification, muft difplay in the moft fubmiffive humility all the circumftances that render his guilt moft deteftable. In the utmoft dejection of foul he muft caft himfelf down before his fovereign judge, addrefs himfelf to his juftice, and acknowledge that he has deferved nothing but difpleafure and indignation, death and punifhment. He muft confefs his tranfgreffions to the Lord, and give himfelf up to the fhame and confufion which the fight of them produces in his fpirit. It muft be a fenfible affliction to him, that he has done wrong to fo good, fo gracious, fo amiable a being; that he has affronted his Creator, his father, and benefactor; that he has tranfgreffed fuch righteous,

righteous, such wise, such reasonable laws; that he has counteracted the great end of his existence, so perverted and degraded his nature, and so far neglected the purposes for which God created him. These considerations must fill him with unfeigned and painful remorse at his sins. They must incite him to take refuge in the mercy of God, and to implore his favour and forgiveness. They must inspire him with a deep abhorrence to all iniquity, a mortal aversion to vice. They must strengthen him in the purpose of quitting the service of sin, and of living to righteousness; and to the execution of this purpose he must now set immediately and earnestly to work. He must effectually cease to do evil, and study to do good. He must settle his conduct on quite other principles and rules; or, in the figurative language of the scriptures, become a *new creature*. Nothing now must be of so much consequence to him, as to combat the unruly desires and

passions

passions that have hitherto had the dominion over him, to fulfill the duties he has hitherto neglected, and to exercise himself in all the virtues, though never so much against his corrupt propensities and his earthly prepossessions. This, this is the essential article of conversion, without which all previous sentiments and practices of repentance will be utterly vain. The unjust must restore the property he obtained by unlawful means to its rightful owner. The unchaste, the adulterer, must burst the chains with which his lusts have bound him, mortify his desires, and cleanse himself from every defilement of flesh and spirit. The avaricious must alter his terrestrial disposition, must learn to regard the treasures of the earth with a generous disdain, and direct his thoughts, his wishes, and desires to invisible things. The haughty must become humble, the rancorous gentle and forgiving, and the worldly become heavenly-minded. Thus must

muſt every one abandon the perverted way he has hitherto walked, forſake the vices and ſins he has hitherto ſerved, avoid all inducements and opportunities to them, and ſtrive after holineſs in the fear of God. This is what God required of his people by the ſon of Amoz. " Waſh ye, ſays he, make you clean; put away the evil of your doings before mine eyes; ceaſe to do evil, learn to do well, ſeek judgement, relieve the oppreſſed, judge the fatherleſs, plead for the widow. Then come, and let us reaſon together, ſaith the Lord: though your ſins be as ſcarlet, they ſhall be white as ſnow; though they be red like crimſon, they ſhall be as wool." Yes, when our converſion is thus effected, when it brings forth the fruits of amendment and righteouſneſs; then may we promiſe ourſelves the greateſt benefits from it.

The ready return of the Prodigal Son was productive of the deſired effects. He
found

found himself not difappointed in his hopes. On the contrary, the kind reception his father gave him far furpaffed all his expectations. No fooner did this tender father defcry his fon, while he was yet a great way off, but he was moved with compaffion towards him. He ran to meet him, fell on his neck, and kiffed him. He forgets all his faults and tranfgreffions. He immediately provides for all his wants. He reftores him to his forfeited right of filiation, fhews him the moft pofitive marks of his paternal clemency and love, and his heart overflows with the livelieft emotions of fatisfaction and joy.—Like as a father pitieth his children, fo the Lord pitieth them that fear him. He is nigh unto them that are of a broken heart, and fave fuch as be of a contrite fpirit. Though he dwell in the high and holy place, yet with him alfo that is of a contrite and humble fpirit, to revive the fpirit of the humble, and to revive the heart of the contrite.

contrite. He looketh on him that is poor and of a contrite spirit, and that trembleth at his word. He is inclined to pity and to spare. He hath no pleasure in the death of the wicked, but that the wicked turn from his way and live. As soon as the sinner draws nigh unto God with a truly repentant heart; as soon as he forsakes his sinful courses, and turns himself wholly to him; so soon does God turn towards him with his grace. He forgives him his sins, he remits the evil consequences of them, he takes him again into favour, and imparts to him, as his son, the free enjoyment of all the goods of his house. And how manifold, how great, are the benefits and blessings this happy alteration and conversion procures him! His guilt is effaced, his sins are done away, his iniquities are pardoned; and shall never be remembered any more. His conscience is restored to peace. God takes a gracious pleasure in him. Access to the throne of grace

grace is open to him, and there he may and will find help and comfort, fo often as they are needful to him. The inhabitants of heaven rejoice at his converfion, they rejoice at having in him a new fharer in their blifs. Heaven is now no longer fhut to him. Death and the grave have laid by their terrors for him. Futurity is no longer dreadful to him. It fhews him the immarceffible crown of glory in the hand of his reconciled judge. It promifes him a felicity which no mortal eye hath feen, which no ear hath heard, and which is above the conception of the human mind. It affures him of the plenitude of joy and a blifsful exiftence at the right-hand of God for ever. In the mean time, till his glorious hopes be fulfilled, the converted man lives more fecurely, as he lives with innocency. Peace and contentment accompany him, fince he has God for his protector and friend, and is confcious of the integrity of his heart. His moral corruption

tion will daily decline, and every victory he gains over it gives him fresh cause to extol the grace of his Redeemer, and to feel the value of his regained freedom. His ability to goodness is ever increasing, and the practice of it grows daily more easy and pleasant. He advances from one degree of perfection to another; his readiness in virtue will be continually improving; and with his virtue, his pleasures and his hopes increase. Happy situation! Ineſtimable advantage! Who would not take all possible pains to obtain it! Who would delay one moment to enter upon the way of repentance and conversion, which alone conducts us to the possession of this felicity! Let us all readily and in ſolemn earneſtneſs resolve upon it. Let us all proceed to put this resolve into immediate execution, and from this inſtant walk the path of virtue and piety with ſtedfaſt perseverance. How bleſſed will then this day have been to us! In what tranquil delight will the reft of our lives flow on! How fedately may we meet our diffolution! How confidently may we expect the glorious recompences that are prepared for the righteous in heaven!

Every thing calls us to hearken to the voice of God, fo lovingly inviting us to repentance and amendment. We yet live to hear this voice. How long it may be allowed us, none of us can tell. Woe to us if we put off from day to day, till it be too late to devote ourfelves obediently to it! Only with him, only in his fervice and in compliance with his commands, is light and life, and joy and felicity, to be found; remote from him, darknefs and bondage, mifery and death, are our only portion. Heavens! into what perils hath fin beguiled us! Let us hafte to efcape from them, and feek grace and help from him who alone can help and fave. Lord, we return to thee, unworthy to be called,
thy

thy fons, but firmly refolved to render oufelves worthy of that glorious name by a better conduct. We are thine, O our Father, thine by creation, and thine by adoption. We will give give ourfelves up to thee as our only proprietor. Thee will we only and conftantly obey. In thee will we feek our whole felicity. O do thou fupply our weaknefs; keep us by thy mighty arm from falling back into fin; grant us to advance in goodnefs, give us to overcome the world, and, by thy fupport, to perfevere unto the end.

thy sons, but their received no tender
caresses: nor any private gracious word by
thence conveyed. We are thine, Thou
knowest thing by creation, and thine by
adoption. We will give ourselves up
to thee as our only proprietor. Thee will
we only and constantly obey. In thee will
we seek our whole felicity. O be thou
firmly our protector; keep us in the
mighty arm from falling back into the
gulph; us to advance in goodness; give us
to overcome the world, and, by thy support, to persevere to the end.

ESTIMATE XXXVI.

THE VALUE OF HUMAN HAPPINESS ITSELF.

The earth is full of thy riches.
Pfalm civ. 24.

ESTIMATE XXXVI.

THE
VALUE
OF
HUMAN HAPPINESS ITSELF.

The earth is full of thy riches.
Psalm civ. 24.

THE VALUE OF HUMAN HAPPINESS ITSELF.

IT is a matter of great confequence to know how to form a right eftimate of human happinefs, or of the ftock of delight and pleafure, of the fum of agreeable fenfations fubfifting among mankind. He that makes the amount of it too great, he that looks on the earth as a paradife, and the prefent ftate of man as a ftate of continued enjoyment, muft be fo often and fo grievoufly deceived in his expectations as to become difpirited and impatient. On the other hand, he who overlooks, if not the whole, yet at least the greatest part of the various benefits that is in the world and amongst mankind, or does not ascribe to it the value it really deserves; he that imagines he perceives, on all sides, nought but imperfection, wretchedness, and want, near and at a distance, around him; who sees, as it were, tears gushing from every human eye, and sighs arising from every human breast; how can he revere the Creator of himself and all men as the all-bountiful Parent of the world! How can he rejoice in his existence, and the existence of his fellow-creatures! How enjoy the advantages and benefits, the agreeablenesses and comforts of life, with a grateful and a chearful heart! And how prejudicial must this be to virtue and piety, to his inward perfection! How negligently at times will he fulfill his duties! How easily will he grow languid and weary in acts of justice and beneficence! We must be on our guard

guard against this gloomy and noxious way of thinking, if we would enjoy our lives, and faithfully discharge the duties of them. Let us not charge God, the best, the most beneficent Existence, the Father of men, with being deficient in kindness. Let us not shut our eyes and our hearts to the beautiful and good that is diffused throughout the world, and distributed among mankind, nor misapply our discernment to the vilification of it. Let us appretiate human happiness for what it actually is, and in the sentiment of its copiousness and magnitude exclaim with the Scripture, " The earth is full of thy riches." Indeed it is difficult, it is even impossible, exactly to weigh the satisfaction and the disgust, the pleasure and the pain, the happiness and the misery, which subsist among mankind, against each other, so as to obtain the just amount of each. This can only be done by him who holds in hand the balance that contains them both, who proportions them

among

mong his creatures according to his good and enlightened will, who poſſeſſes both in his almighty mind, and perceives all their poſſible and actual effects in every event. We may, however, form a juſter eſtimate of human happineſs than is uſually done. We may ſurvey it on many ſides but little noticed, and call our attention to many collateral circumſtances and things which we probably have hitherto overlooked. May I offer you a few ſuggeſtions on the proper evaluation of human happineſs? To this end I ſhall do two things:

First, lay before you ſome conſiderations on the nature and magnitude of human happineſs in general; and

Then deliver you a few rules for rightly apprétiating it in particular occurrences.

There is, abſolutely, happineſs among mankind. Of this, our own experience,
of

of this, what we see and observe in regard to others, will not permit us to harbour a doubt. For, how can we refuse to say, We and other men have various agreeable conceptions and sensations; we see, hear, feel, think, and perform many things with satisfaction and delight; we and others frequently enjoy pleasure and gladness; we and others are often contented with our condition, and we are comfortable in the consciousness and contemplation of it? And is not all this, when taken together, happiness?

Indeed human happiness is not unmixed; it is not perfectly pure. Not one of us all possesses purely agreeable conceptions and sensations; no one enjoys pure pleasures and delights; no one is perfectly and at all times satisfied with whatever he is and does, and with every thing that befalls him; no one experiences purely desireable occurrences. To every person is distributed his measure of dislike, of dis-

pleasure

pleasure and pain from adverse events. Every one must taste of the cup of sorrow as well as of the goblet of joy. Even our most agreeable representations and feelings are adulterated with a greater or less commixture of ingredients that are distasteful and bitter. But this is the necessary and unavoidable consequence of our nature, and the present constitution of things; and so must it be, unless it were proper for man to be dazzled by happiness and intoxicated with joy.

As human happiness is not unalloyed, so neither is it uninterrupted. It does not fill up each day, each hour, each moment of our earthly existence. As light and darkness alternately succeed each other in the natural world, so likewise in the moral, but much seldomer, bad days succeed to good, and misery to happiness. Pleasure and pain, joys and sorrows, tread very closely on each other; often suddenly interchange,

change, and often arife from each other. Exceffive pleafure becomes pain; immoderate joy turns into forrow; fuper-abundant happinefs frequently weighs its' poffeffor down to the ground. Our connections with outward things, their relation to us, and their influences upon us, are not always the fame, may to-morrow be quite different from what they yefterday were; and thefe very things are all fluctuating, tranfitory, and of fhort duration. So far as our happinefs is built on outward things, fo far muft it be frequently interrupted. And even in ourfelves, in our train of thought and difpofitions, in our own mutability, are caufes already fufficient to prevent its confifting in a ftated, firm, and linked feries of pure agreeable reprefentations and feelings.

Human happinefs is, thirdly, not equally great to all men, and cannot be fo. All cannot inhabit the fame zone, and enjoy the same goods and the same amenities; all cannot have the same education, be invested with the same station, carry on the same business, or attain to the same degree of politeness and intelligence. All have not the same disposition and aptitude for pursuing, for finding and for enjoying, a certain greater proportion, or certain nobler kinds of happiness; as all have not the same attentive and regulated understanding, the same formed and refined taste, the same sentimental and participating heart. All, in fine, do not conduct themselves in the same manner; and but too many think and act in such a way as if they were determined by no means to be happy, but ever to become more wretched. As great, therefore, as the difference is between all these circumstances and things, so great must likewise be the difference of the portions of happiness among mankind.

But

But even the same person is not always equally sensible to the happiness allotted him, nor always alike satisfied with it. Time and enjoyment but too often weaken the sentiment of the goods we possess. Little uneasinesses and vexations not unfrequently deprive all the advantages and comforts we have in our power of their value. And, then, neither our body nor our mind is constantly attuned to the same lively and vigorous sensations, as to enable us to enjoy, with consciousness to enjoy, the beautiful and the good within us, and without us, at all times alike. And this arises partly from the degree of our natural sensibility, and partly from the particular humour and temper of mind in which we are at the time.

But though human happiness be neither unmingled, nor uninterrupted, nor equally great, for every man, nor even to its possessor equally sensible and satisfying at all times;

times; yet it is still real, it is manifold; it is great, abundantly great; it is capable of a constantly progressive augmentation; four particulars that will place its nature and value in a clear point of view.

It is real. Human happiness is neither fancy, nor imposture, nor self-deceit. It is founded on representations and feelings, of which we are as positively and intimately conscious as we are of our existence and our life; and when these representations and feelings are agreeable, when they occasion us satisfaction and pleasure, then no man will make it a matter of dispute, that it is well with us, that we are more or less happy. And where is he that has not had, that has not frequently had such representations and feelings, and has not felt himself happy in the consciousness of them? Human happiness will also stand the test of reflection and consideration. It is not the work of deception, not an agreeable dream, that

that on our awaking vanishes away. It does not shun serenity and silence, willingly takes reason for its companion, and always remains what it previously was. Nay, only under these circumstances does it appear to the thinking and sentimental man in its full capacity and its real greatness. Recount, O man, recount, in some peaceful and serious hour of life, all the benefits thou possessest, and which endow thy mind, thy person, and thy outward station; all the advantages in temporals and spirituals thou hast and mayst acquire; all the pleasures and delights thou enjoyest, and art capable of enjoying; all the good that is in thee, and is effected by thy means; all the prospects into a better futurity that lie open before thee: reckon all these together, examine them as severely, as impartially, as thou wilt; ask thyself whether these benefits are not real benefits, these advantages not real advantages, these pleasures and delights not real pleasures and delights,

delights, this good not actually good, these prospects not desireable and consoling; and if thou canst not deny it, then it remains clear, that the happiness flowing from them is real happiness.

No less diversified is human happiness than it is real. It is as diversified as the necessities, the capacities, the inclinations, the behaviour, the temper, the circumstances, of mankind require. A thousand kinds of benefit and advantage are common to us all; a thousand sources of satisfaction and pleasure stand open to us all. Are we not all enlightened by the same sun? Are we not all cheared by its light and its heat? Are not the beauties of nature displayed before us all in their splendour and glory? Are we not all transported with the view of them, when we regard and observe them? Does not every thing that lives and moves inspire us with joy, when we open our ears and our hearts to its

its voice? Does not every thing elevate our spirit to the Creator and Father of the world, and invite us to praise him as the all-bountiful God? Do we not all find the most agreeable, most delicious taste in the food and the drinks which his providence has granted us for our recreation and refreshment? Are we not susceptible of innumerable agreeable sensible impressions and feelings? Are not thousands and thousands of the creatures of the universe of service to us all? Are not the earth, water, air, fire, are not all the powers of nature devoted to our welfare, and employed in the advancement of it? Are we not a thousand times gladdened by the shining sky, the mild refreshing breeze, the field cloathed with food and smiling with plenty, the tree fragrant with blossoms or laden with fruits, the shady forest, the limpid stream, the moving joy of every living thing? And how variegated is the pleasure we all enjoy! Do we not all enjoy the pleasure of life and of free and voluntary motion; the pleasure of thought and consideration, of investigation and discovery; the pleasure of labour and of rest; of prudent designs, and of their succesful execution; the pleasure of the retired enjoyment of ourselves, and of social converse with others; the pleasure of received or afforded assistance; the pleasure of cautiously avoided or of heroically conquered danger; the pleasure of love and of friendship; the pleasure of rational adoration and devotion? What sources of happiness! How different, and yet how rich and general! From whom are they totally debarred? What man has not used them? Who may not daily draw from these wells of pleasure? And how various must the happiness be that is daily drawn from them!—Does not each age, each sex, each station, each course of life, each charge, each connection; does not every season of the year, every climate, every country, every

every greater or smaller society, procure from them its peculiar advantages, pleasures and joys, its own causes of agreeable sensations, of happiness? And who, amid this diversity of sources and means of pleasure and good, go empty away? Who, but by his own fault, can be wholly unhappy? No; Lord, the earth is full of thy riches!

If human happiness be various, so likewise is it great, abundantly great. Great in regard of the multitude of agreeable sensations; great in regard of the vivacity and strength, as well as of the continuance of them. Who can enumerate the agreeable conceptions and sensations, which only one man has in one year, which only one man has in the whole course of his life? Who is able to reckon up the multitude of agreeable ideas and sensations which at once exist in all living men in every hour, in every moment. To what a sum of happiness must the whole result amount! And how often do thefe fenfations proceed to tranfport! How often do they burft forth in tears of joy, in hearty mirth, in fhouts of jubilation! And how often do whole years, and ftill longer periods of life, glide away in calm fatisfaction to a man, wherein he conftantly feels pleafed with his exiftence, and finds no caufe of diffatisfaction or complaint! Indeed, at fuch times, a thoufand forts of unpleafant reprefentations and feelings take place among mankind; indeed, at the fame time the tears of pain and forrow are flowing from a thoufand and a thoufand eyes: but if this feem to diminifh the bulk of human happinefs, yet does it not remove it; it ftill remains not only great, but preponderatively great. Where is the man, who, in the aggregate, has had more difagreeable than agreeable reprefentations and feelings, that has experienced more pain than pleafure? And if there be fuch perfons, how fmall is their number in comparifon with the number of

thofe

those that have had the contrary to rejoice in! No; the exceeding weight of happiness above that of misery is great; and so sure as that there is more life than death, more health than sickness, more superfluity and satiety than hunger and want, more free and unimpeded exhibition of mental and bodily powers than total inaction or painful restriction of them, more love than hatred, more hope than fear, more desire for prolongation of life than for its abbreviation, amongst mankind! No; for one mournful hour we pass in sighs, we may composedly and chearfully live an hundred; for one tear forced out by pain, we may shed a thousand tears of generous sensibility, or of sedate and pious joy; for one misfortune that happens to us, a thousand of known and unknown benefits fall to our lot.

Lastly, human happiness is capable of an ever progressive increase. And this uncommonly

commonly exalts its worth; this puts all complaint of ſhort ſorrows and tranſient miſery to ſilence. Human happineſs is not confined to the narrow limits of this life; it is immortal, like the man that enjoys it. The happineſs we here enjoy, enjoy as rational and good beings, is the path to ſtill purer and higher happineſs in a better world; and the enjoyment of that renders us capable of the enjoyment of this purer and ſuperior happineſs. Let, therefore, human happineſs be never ſo much alloyed at preſent, never ſo much interrupted, never ſo much circumſcribed, what an importance, what a ſweetneſs muſt it give to the proſpect of its never ceaſing, but always continuing, always improving, always becoming greater and more perfect, and at length actually vanquiſhing all evil and miſery!

Theſe are the general ideas which reaſon and experience give us of the nature and magni-

magnitude of human happiness. Allow me to subjoin a few rules for rightly appretiating and judging of it in particular incidents, or in regard to particular persons.

Wouldst thou, then, my friend and my brother, wouldst thou justly pronounce on the value of human happiness in particular incidents, and poize it against human misery; then do not confound prosperity and happiness together. Do not argue from the defect of the one to the want of the other. That is far more rare than this: that consists in outward advantages and goods that adorn us, and are sometimes beneficial to us, and sometimes hurtful; this, in images of the mind and sensations of the heart, which procure us satisfaction and pleasure; that is not in our power, this depends greatly on ourselves: both may subsist of themselves; they are often divided asunder; and as prosperity is not
always

always attended by happiness, so neither is the former a necessary requisite of the latter. Indeed, if only the rich, the eminent, the great, the mighty, only such as are surrounded by splendour and opulence, only them that fare sumptuously every day, and pass their lives in tumultuous pleasures, are to be and accounted happy, then wilt thou find but little happiness amongst the sons of men; for, comparatively, but a few can be rich and eminent, and great and mighty; but a few can distinguish themselves from others by pomp and splendour, or by a luxurious and voluptuous life. But, if there be but few such darlings of fortune, then are there so many more happy, so many more chearful and contented men; and whom thou mayst find in every station, among all the classes of mankind; whom thou mayst and wilt very often find in the meanest cottage of the countryman, in the unornamented habitation of the workman, not unfrequently in

the

the tattered garb of poverty, and under the squallid appearance of wretchedness.

Wouldst thou, farther, judge rightly of human happiness in particular instances; then take as much care, on the other hand, not to account misfortune and unhappiness as one and the same, or always, from the presence of the one, to conclude on the presence of the other. No; misfortune does not always imply, does not imply unhappiness with wise and good persons; and our heavenly Father, who has ordained us to happiness, has so constituted our nature, and the nature of things, that we may experience much misfortune, and yet be happy, and still rejoice in his bounty, and in our present and future existence. Let it be, that, by untoward events, I suffer loss in my property, in my outward distinctions, in my health, in my fame, that some sources of my pleasure fail, that my friends and intimates forsake me; let it be, that

that all this shakes the stem of my happiness, that it weakens and brings it to the ground; is it therefore wholly and for ever destroyed and overthrown? May it not still, like the tree which has been bent by the storm to the earth, lift up its head again, and again be rich in blossoms and fruits, when the tempest is over and gone, and serenity and peace are once more restored? Have I, then, by these adverse events, lost all the agreeable images and feelings I formerly had? With these outwards goods and advantages, am I then likewise despoiled of my inward spiritual perfection, and the consciousness of what I am, and shall hereafter be? Am I, then, degraded from my affinity with God and the future world, which afforded me so much comfort and repose? Do not, then, a thousand other sources of delight and joy still stand open to me? Do not time and reflection and business heal the most painful wounds inflicted by misfortune?—

Beware,

Beware, then, of suppoſing every unfortunate man to be unhappy! Misfortune is tranſitory: happineſs can ſtand out a thouſand attacks of it, ere it can be eradicated from the ſpot where it has once taken root. On the ſame principle, beware too of always ſuppoſing trouble and miſery to be where thou feeſt tears to flow. They flow as often, and probably oftener, from ſources of delight than of pain; and we have commonly mingled ſenſations, in which the diſagreeable is far over-balanced by the pleaſant; ſenſations ariſing from the moſt cordial feelings of benevolence and affection to the human race, of virtue and greatneſs of mind, and not unfrequently are connected with the moſt enchanting recollections of bleſſings already enjoyed, and with the moſt delightful proſpects of future bliſs.

Wouldſt thou, thirdly, my chriſtian brother, judge rightly of human happineſs in particular cafes, and in regard of particular perfons, and not overlook the greater proportion of it; then do not dwell merely, not principally on the extraordinarily fhining kinds and difplays of happinefs, which attract the eye of every beholder,—the world indeed is not fo prolific of them,—but take likewife, and ftill more, into confideration, the placid, domeftic pleafures and joys which lie concealed from the world. Bring into the account the conftantly remaining advantages and benefits a man enjoys, though becaufe of their being conftant, they excite in him no very ftrong emotions of joy and delight. But feldom can we enjoy the lively pleafure of returning health and of reftored life; but daily the quiet pleafure of the uninterrupted continuance of both. But feldom are we able to bring great matters to effect, rarely tafte the fuavity of being the benefactor and the redeemer of our brother; but daily may we comfort and

chear

chear ourselves in the reflection on having performed something good and useful in our station and calling. But rarely can we accomplish such remarkable and desirable alterations in our condition, as shall fill us with a peculiar and hitherto unknown delight; but daily may we enjoy the innumerable agreeablenesses and advantages of it. But seldom can we, probably, partake of public diversions, more rarely approach the bright and dazzling lustre of the fashionable circles of persons far above us in rank; but daily may we enjoy the pleasures of domestic life, of familiar intercourse, and friendly conversation of our own, walk daily in the genial light which peace and satisfaction shed around us. But seldom, perhaps, does our devotion kindle into transport; but daily may it procure us comfort, and repose, and tranquil joy. And is not that, is not even this to be called happiness? Shall the good and the agreeable that we may so often,

often, that we may daily enjoy, lose its value for the very reason that it so often, that it daily procures us satisfaction and pleasure? Ought not this circumstance to render it so much the more precious to us? Does it not therefore contribute so much the more to the sum of our agreeable representations and feelings, and therefore to our happiness?

Would'st thou, fourthly, my christian brother, rightly appreciate and rightly judge of human happiness, and that especially in regard of particular cases and persons; then consider man not merely as a sensual, but likewise as a spiritual and moral creature, and take also into the account the benefits, the advantages, the pleasures, he enjoys as such. Or have we only then agreeable representations and feelings, are we happy only then, when our senses procure us pleasure and delight, when our appetites are flattered, when our

animal

animal neceffities are fatisfied, when we feel and enjoy the value of health, of bodily ftrength, of riches, and outward welfare? Are we not as much, and more fo, as often as we apply our mental faculties with confcioufnefs, and not without fuccefsful effects; as often as we meditate on important matters, or matters we hold to be important; as often as we difcover any traces of truth; as often as we adjuft or increafe our knowledge of whatever kind? Are we not alfo happy as often as we feel the dignity of our nature, the greatnefs of our vocation, our bleffed connection with the Deity; as often as we maintain, like free and rational beings, the dominion over ourfelves, and over the things that are without us; as often as we thence obtain a victory over evil; as often as we obferve that we draw near to chriftian perfection? Are we not fo, as often as we form a good defign, or bring it to effect; as often as we are actuated by benevolence and love towards others; as often as we are employed in beneficence; as often as we have completed a useful work, or honestly discharged our duty? Are we not so even then when we sacrifice something to duty and to virtue, or to the common interest; when we bear and suffer for others from magnanimity or friendship; when we endure adversity and misfortunes with fortitude, and become wiser and better by them? Oh, how much more contented, how much more happy is, frequently, the obscure, but reflecting and virtuous moralist, the suffering but pious christian, than the opulent and dignified voluptuary, who is all flesh, and knows no other pleasures than what his senses procure him! How much more real and lasting pleasure does often one hour of calm and lucid contemplation on important objects, and the sedate enjoyment of our mental powers, afford us, than whole days of noisy and tumultuous joys! How much more

more does one generous or beneficial deed contribute to our satisfaction, than the rushing torrents of sensual amusements, which quickly pass away! And yet how seldom are these purer pleasures, these sublimer joys, brought into the account, in taking estimates of human happiness!

Would'st thou lastly, O man, evaluate properly thy own and thy brother's happiness; then consider the human creature not barely in certain epochas or times, but in the whole capacity of his life and fortunes. Connect the past, the present, and the future, so together in thy thoughts, as in the nature of things they are connected together. If this or that period of the life of a man appears cloudy and wretched, another will cast the more light upon it, and evince more happiness enjoyed. Oft is the first entrance on affairs, in active life, difficult and toilsome, and its progress brings comfort and pleasure. Sometimes youth,

youth, and sometimes manhood, is wealthier in happiness. Often is there more enjoyment in this life, often more qualification and preparation for future enjoyment. Would'ft thou ftate the fum of thy own or thy brother's happinefs; then fet all thefe againft each other, reckon all agreeable and chearful fenfations together, the innocent fportive delights of childhood, the livelier joys of youth, the more rational, nobler pleafures of the manly and advanced age. Think on all thou haft enjoyed, and ftill enjoyeft, of agreeable and good, and alfo what thou mayft hope to enjoy in future; on all that thou art, and haft, and doth, that is good and profitable, and that thou mayft and will be, and have, and do, in all fucceeding times. Forget not that thou art immortal, that thou art ordained to everlafting happinefs, that thou art already happy in hope; and, from the firft fruits, conclude of the full harveft; from the fweets of the foretafte,

of

of the deliciousness of complete fruition. These rules will guide thee safely in appretiating human happiness, and enable thee to perceive its true nature and magnitude.

On the whole, my christian brother, conclude, that man was not made for misery by his Creator and father, but was formed for happiness; that to this end he is endowed with dispositions and capacities for it; that he finds in himself and without him the most various and abundant sources of satisfaction and pleasure; and that it is almost always his own fault when he does not draw from them contentment and joy. Farther conclude, that human happiness is no insignificant, contemptible matter, as the unfortunate and the melancholy at times represent it to be, and that none but the misanthropist can wholly be blind to it, none but the slight and thoughtless can hold it for a trifling object. And assuredly conclude, that there is far, far more agreeable than disagreeable sensation, far more happiness than misery among mankind, far, far more good than evil in the world. In fine, exalt this comfortable idea by just and vigorous reflection: that in the kingdom of God, the God of love, happiness will always abide, and be always augmenting and spreading; and that, on the other hand, misery will be ever diminishing, and at length will cease, and be succeeded by perfection and bliss. So wilt thou think worthily of God, and justly of the state and appointment of man. So wilt thou be always chearful in the present life, and be constantly more fitted or the future.

ESTIMATE XXXVII.

RULES

FOR

RIGHTLY APPRETIATING

THE

VALUE of THINGS.

There be many that say, Who will shew us any good?   Psalm iv. 6.

RULES

RULES

FOR

RIGHTLY APPRETIATING

THE

VALUE OF THINGS.

A Man may possess a variety of goods, enjoy many pleasures, acquire many advantages, seek and obtain many kinds of perfection and happiness; but all of them are not of equal value, and rarely can a man possess and enjoy them all, and much seldomer all in the same proportion or degree. These goods, these pleasures,

sures, these advantages, these kinds of perfection and happiness, are not always compatible with each other. The obtaining and the possessing of one frequently militates with the possession and the acquisition of another. The one frequently cannot be purchased or acquired without the loss or the voluntary sacrifice of the other. There are cases where I can neither duly edify and perfectionate my spirit, nor enjoy the pleasure arising from the proper discharge of my duty, without weakening my body and hurting my health; cases wherein I cannot maintain and secure peace of conscience and comfort of heart, without manifest loss of many earthly advantages; cases wherein I must chuse between the acceptance of God and the approbation and esteem of men, between inward perfection concealed from the notice of the world and outward splendid distinctions, between sensible and spiritual pleasures, between present and future happiness; and must relinquish

quish one for the sake of the other. For men who do not act upon firm principles, who do not take wisdom, and virtue, and piety, for their guides, are very liable in such cases to be confused, and to fall into mistake. The less a man knows of the value of things; the more he suffers himself to be dazzled by outside appearance and shew; and the more wavering his sentiments and inclinations are, so much the more unsteady will he be in this election; and so much the oftener will he prefer the evil to the good, the worse to the better. To guard you against this tormenting and dangerous uncertainty, and to furnish you with sure motives of determination in such cases, is the scope of my present address.

We have already, on various occasions, discussed the principal objects that relate to human happiness, or such as are generally held to be so; we have investigated the benefit and advantage of life, of health,

of

of riches, of honour, of sensible, of spiritual pleasure, of piety, of virtue, of devotion, of religion, of public worship; we have animadverted on the advantages of solitary, of social, of busy, of rural, of domestic happiness, of friendship, of liberty, of learning, and others; and we have found that they all in and for themselves deserve our regard and esteem, that they all more or less contribute to our happiness. Let us now compare these things together, or see which of them we must prefer to the other, which we are to sacrifice or relinquish for the sake of the other, when we cannot obtain, or possess them at once. Wilt thou proceed safely in thy choice, O my christian brother? Then let the following rules and decisive arguments be the guides of thy conduct therein.

In the first place, remember to prefer the necessary to the agreeable and convenient. That is the foundation of happiness;

ness; this a part of the structure thou art to erect upon it. Of that thou canst not be deprived, but thou must be miserable; the want of this does but lessen thy prosperity and thy pleasure. It is agreeable to increase riches, and to live in opulence; but necessary to have an unsullied conscience, and neither to be afraid before God nor man. It is agreeable to be esteemed by all men; but necessary to be assured of the good-pleasure of God, and to be satisfied with one's self. It is agreeable to acquire a various and extensive knowledge of all that can content and gratify the inquisitive mind; but necessary to be concerned about a fundamental and thorough knowledge of the affairs of our station and calling. It is agreeable to form various connections with many other people, and to enlarge our sphere of action; but necessary to answer conscientiously the demands of the closer connections in which we stand, as parents, as spouses, as citizens, and to
be

be active and useful in the narrower circle wherein Providence has placed us. It is agreeable to live long, and in the enjoyment of a blooming health; but necessary to live virtuously, and piously, and generally useful. It is agreeable to be decked with outward distinctions, and to be surrounded with a certain splendour; but necessary to acquire intrinsic perfection, and to provide for its constant improvement. It is convenient to be free from all kinds of constraint, to follow one's inclinations of every sort, to have others at one's service, and to divide one's time between pleasure and repose; but necessary to discharge faithfully the duties of our station and calling, and to repay, by reciprocal service, the services we receive from society. All the former we may dispense with, and not be unhappy; but with the latter not. Prefer, therefore, in all cases, what is necessary, that without which thou canst not be happy, to what is merely agreeable and

con-

convenient, what merely in certain refpects increafes or raifes thy happinefs; prefer a good confcience to all riches; the being well-pleafing to God, to all human applaufe; the knowledge neceffary to thy poft and calling, to every other kind of knowledge; thy domeftic and civil connections and relationfhips, to all other connections and relationfhips; a virtuous and generally ufeful, to the longeft and healthieft life without virtue and general utility; thy intrinfic perfection, to all outward diftinctions; thy duty, to all conveniences and independency: be ready to facrifice all thefe with joy whenever thou art reduced to chufe between them. The former are neceffary and effential to thy happinefs; of the latter thou canft be deprived and yet be happy.

Prize, farther, if thou would'ft rightly judge and chufe, prize thofe benefits and advantages which thou haft thyfelf acquired

quired as the confequences and recompence of thy wife and good behaviour, at a much higher rate than fuch as have fallen to thee, without thy procuring and without thy defert, by means of fome favourable concurrence of outward things, even though they may be in and for themfelves far greater and more brilliant than the former. A moderate livelihood, that thou haft earned by prudence and honeft fkill, by affiduity and labour; is of far more value than the greateft riches thou haft inherited, or haft acquired by any fortunate occurrence. The loweft dignity, the moft inconfiderable importance, to which thou art raifed by thy own exertions and alertnefs, and the fervices thou haft rendered to fociety, confers upon thee more real honour than whatever brilliancy furrounds thee by thy birth, or that can reverberate upon thee from the high and mighty with whom thou art connected. The fuperiority of mind and heart, which thou mayeft confider consider as the fruit of thy virtuous conflicts, of thy unremitted struggles after higher perfection, must be dearer to thee than all the gifts and talents, though never so great, for which thou art indebted to nature or the first rudiments of education; the testimony of a good conscience, founded on the inward sentiment of thy integrity, and which is the recompence of thy blameless and prudent conduct; must be of more account with thee than the flattering approbation and the loudest applause of men, who seldom know thee thoroughly, and, who for the most part, judge more from semblance than from reality. The esteem and affection shewn thee on thy own account, on account of what thou actually art and dost, which is bestowed upon thee as an intelligent and good man, as a useful member of society, must be of far more worth to thee than the profoundest civilities exhibited to thee on account of thy quality, thy office, or thy wealth. For all the goods and diftinctions that accrue to thee more from thyfelf than from fortune, thou canft neither obtain nor preferve without the ufe and application of thy nobler capacities and powers, without becoming actually wifer and better, and more perfect; and this wifdom, this moral benefit, this perfection, remains with thee for ever, abides by thee even then when thou haft loft all thofe outward goods and privileges, when thou paffeft over into a ftate wherein they will no longer avail, and poffefs any worth no more.

Prefer, thirdly, O my Chriftian brother, who would'ft form a right judgement of the goods, the pleafures, the advantages of this life, of what belongs or is held to belong to human happinefs, and would'ft chufe from amongft thefe things like a wife man, prefer that which is in thy power to thofe things which do not depend on thee, but purely on outward circumftances, and incidental

dental caufes. After the former thou wilt not ftrive in vain; they are what thou mayft affuredly, thou mayft conftantly have and enjoy: whereas, in purfuit of the latter, thou wilt frequently throw away thy time and diffipate thy faculties, and wilt never be fure of their continuance. It is in thy power to maintain an authority over thy-felf, to fhake off the yoke of error, of prejudice, and of moral fervitude; but it depends not on thee whether thou fhalt rule over others, or be in fubferviency to them; whether thou fhalt be invefted with the fupreme command, or fill the place of a fubject. It is in thy power, by a wife behaviour and a chriftian temper, to fecure tranquillity and contentednefs of heart; but it depends not on thee to enjoy the fortune of wealth, of might, or of exalted ftation. It is in thy power to cultivate thy mind, to purify and to improve thy heart; but it depends not on thee to render thy outward circumftances as flourifhng and brilliant as thou would'ſt defire. It is in thy power to do what thy poſt and thy calling exact with conſciencioufneſs and integrity; but it depends not on thee to effect fo much good by it about thee, and to have fo much influence on the general welfare, as thou earneſtly would'ſt. It is in thy power to diſtinguiſh thyſelf above others by ſincerity and virtue; but it depends not always on thee to exalt thyſelf over them by extraordinary gifts and abilities, or by peculiar defert. It is in thy power to enjoy the complacency of God, thy eternal Sovereign and Judge, and to rejoice in his favour; but it depends not on thee to obtain the applauſe of thy contemporaries, or to ſecure the favour of the great and potent of the earth. It is in thy power to gain the love of thy fellow-creatures by gentleneſs, kindneſs, and beneficence; but it depends not on thee to be reverenced, admired, or promoted by them, or even to be eſteemed and rewarded accord-

according to thy merits. It is, finally, in thy power to live virtuously and piously, and thereby to prepare thyself for a superior state; but it depends not on thee to perform a great and shining part on the theatre of this world, or to attain to the extremest pinnacle of the age of man. Consume not, therefore, thy time and thy powers in striving after goods, after eminencies, after pleasures, that do not depend on thee, and which as often and still oftener fall to the lot of those who have never sought nor deserved them, than to such as have earned them, and to whom they are due; but apply them to what is in thy power; so wilt thou never employ them in vain, and thy aim, thy felicity, will infallibly be thy reward.

Prefer, fourthly, if thou would'st judiciously determine between the objects that relate to human happiness, or are reckoned of that number, prefer activity to rest.

Reſt, inactive reſt, is properly only defect, only limitation, only effect and indication of weakneſs. Activity alone is life, is enjoyment, is happineſs. The more active thou art, and the more prudent, the more beneficial thy activity is; ſo much the more perfect art thou, ſo much the more do'ſt thou reſemble the Deity. Wilt thou then triumph in exiſtence, wilt thou be happy, and happy in an eminent degree; then ſtrive not after reſt as thy object, but enjoy it only as the means to greater activity; and prefer always that which occupies thy faculties in a proportionate degree, and which promiſes to thee recompence and enjoyment after labour and toil, to that which leaves thy powers unemployed, which ſinks thee into ſloth, and promiſes thee pleaſure and benefit at no expence whatever. Think therefore for thyſelf, and decline not ſtudy and reſearch, rather than barely let others think for thee, and ſimply repoſe in their opinions and decrees.

Rather

Rather labour thyself, and by labouring exercise thy talents, than merely let others labour for thee, and enjoy the fruits of their labours in indolent repose. Prefer a busy mode of life, an office, a trust, that keeps thy mind in greater activity, and leaves thee little leisure, to any other mode of life, to any other charge that employs thee but little, or not at all, even though this be far more profitable and considerable than the other. Prize the pleasure that is the natural fruit of thy reflection and industry, that thou hast purchased with labour and toil, in the sweat of thy brow, far before any other presented thee by chance, and which thou mayst simply enjoy, without any previous preparation and any desert of thy own. The former will render thee far more perfect, far more contented and happy, than the latter; and no endeavours, no toil is lost, which conduces to this end; but thou wilt find it gain, and gain abiding by thee, when the languor

guor of inactive repose, and its surfeiting enjoyment, leaves thee nothing but melancholy reflections behind.

Would'ft thou, fifthly, my chriftian brother, learn rightly to deem of the goods, the privileges, the pleafures, that conftitute human happinefs, or are reckoned among its properties, and would'ft chufe between them as a prudent man; then prefer what is fpiritual to that which is fenfible, that which renders thy fpirit more contented and perfect, to fuch as procure thee pleafure and delight by means of thy fenfes alone, or promotes thy outward welfare. Animal life, health, and vigour of body, riches in earthly goods, are undoubtedly defireable things; but fpiritual life, the health and ftrength of the foul, riches in knowledge, in wifdom, and in virtue, are far, far more defireable. Thofe may as eafily become prejudicial as profitable to us; may as probably render us wretched

as

as happy, and a thousand accidents may deprive us of them; these are and constantly remain to be real goods; can never be of detriment to us; render us continually and for ever happy. Those are without us, do not necessarily belong to ourselves; are only connected with us for a longer or a shorter time: these belong essentially to self, are indissolubly connected with us, and subsist as long as we subsist ourselves. Never hesitate, then, to sacrifice the health of thy body to the health and the life of thy soul, the riches that consist in gold and silver to the riches of wisdom and virtue, thy outward circumstances to thy inward perfection, if thou art obliged to chuse from between them, if thou canst not possess and preserve them together. They are only the occasions, the means of happiness: these are happiness itself. Beware of preferring the means to the end, or of striving as earnestly after them as after these. Station, rank, might, and

and power, are certainly brilliant distinctions; but a cultivated understanding, preserved integrity, uncorrupted faith, pious, christian dispositions, a pure heart, a blameless, beneficent life, greater similarity to Jesus, greater similarity to God, are far, far more valuable distinctions. They belong to thy outward condition, and change immediately with it: these adorn thy spirit, and are, like thyself, immortal. Let not them then, but these be the ultimate aim of thy endeavours and desires. Sensual pleasures are undoubtedly real pleasures, and, when they are moderate and harmless, are worthy of thy wishes and thy proportionate endeavours: but far purer, far nobler still are the pleasures of the mind and the heart; the pleasure which the knowledge of truth, the discharge of our duty, beneficence towards our brother, advancement in goodness, fellowship with God, and gladness in him, the animating prospect of a better life. The former we hold

hold in common with the beasts of the field; the latter connect us with superior existences, and with the Deity himself. Those frequently leave heaviness, disgust, and pain behind them; these are as beneficial as innocent, and never lose of their value nor their sweets. Therefore let them not hinder thee in the acquisition and enjoyment of these; let not sensuality, but reason, be thy guide in the selection of thy pleasures; prize that which satisfies and chears thy mind and thy heart far above all that flatters thy senses; and make no hesitation to offer up these when thou canst not enjoy them both. So wilt thou prefer reality to appearance, the essential to the agreeable, and fix thy happiness on a solid basis.

Wilt thou, lastly, rightly appretiate the advantages, the pleasures that relate to human happiness, and discreetly chuse between them, in cases where they cannot subsist

subsist together; then prefer the lasting to the transient, the eternal to the temporal. Thou wishest, not merely for a few days or years, thou wishest to be happy for ever. Seek therefore thy happiness, not in what lasts only for a few days or years, and then vanishes away; seek it principally in such objects as are untransitory and ever abiding. All outward things, that now favour and please and delight thee, are transitory, and of short duration; only thy inward perfection, the perfection of thy spirit, remains for ever. What is more uncertain than the possession of riches? What more transient than earthly elevation, than the respect and the honour of men? What is more deceitful than their favour? What is more fleeting and vain than sensual pleasure? What is more perishable than health and strength, than life itself? To what accidents, what changes, and revolutions, are not all these advantages and possessions liable? Who can confide in them but for a year, a year, but for a day, but for an hour, with perfect assurance? And how inevitable is, sooner or later, their total loss! Nothing of them all will remain with thee in death and in the grave; nothing of all these will accompany thee into eternity; nothing of all these will retain even the smallest value in that better world to which thou art hastening! No; thither thou wilt be only attended by thy spiritual advantages, thy good dispositions and actions; there nothing will avail thee but wisdom and virtue, and integrity, a sound understanding, a well ordered heart, and a happy dexterity in doing what is lawful and right. These, alone, are lasting advantages and possessions; advantages and possessions that are not subject to the revolutions of things, which neither death nor the grave can ravish from thee. Learnest thou here to think rationally and nobly; learnest thou here to govern thyself, to conquer thy lusts; learnest thou here to use all thy faculties

culties and powers according to his will who gave them to thee, and to the good of thy brother; learneſt thou to love God above all things, and thy neighbour as thyſelf; acquireſt thou here an abundant, effective inclination to all that is right and good, to all that is beautiful and great; doſt thou make at preſent the diſcharge of thy duty thy joy, and beneficence thy pleaſure? Then art thou happy, and wilt remain ſo for ever, even though thou art neither rich, nor great, nor powerful, nor healthy, nor vigorous, nor liveſt long. Oh, then, forget not that all viſible things, however brilliant and charming, are tranſient, and only remain for a little while; but that thy ſpirit is immortal, that thy future appointment is great, that this life is only a preparation for a higher, and that therefore, in regard to thy real felicity, thy whole concern is this, that thou advance the perfection of thy ſpirit, anſwer to thy great

great vocation, and render thyfelf capable and worthy of that fuperior life.

And thefe are the points of difcrimination, thefe the rules that muft guide us in our judgement and our choice of the objects which relate to human happinefs, or are reckoned for fuch, and will certainly guide us aright. If, in regard to all the goods, the affairs, the advantages, the pleafures and joys of this life, we prefer the neceffary to the merely convenient and agreeable, what we acquire by reflection and fkill to what accident and fortune beftow, what is in our power to what does not depend upon us; if we prefer activity to reft, the fpiritual to the fenfible, the lafting to the tranfient, and eternals to temporals; then fhall we make no ftep in vain on the way that leads to happinefs, and as certainly lay our hand on the glorious prize, as we purfue that way.

[illegible] perfection, and rendering himself capable of that superior life.

And little are the points of distinction, [illegible] the rules of [illegible] guiding our judgment and our choice of the objects which relate to human happiness, or are reckoned for such, and will certainly guide us aright, in regard to all the goods, the affairs, the advantages, the pleasures and joys of this life, if we prefer the necessary to the merely convenient and agreeable, what we acquire by reflection and art, to what accident and fortune bestow, what is in our power to what does not depend upon us; if we prefer actively to rely the spiritual to the sensual; the lasting to the transient, the eternal to temporary; then shall we make no step in vain on the way that leads to happiness, and we certainly lay our hand on the greatest prize we pursue [illegible].

THE
VANITY
OF ALL
EARTHLY THINGS.

Vanity of vanities, faith the preacher, vanity of vanities, all is vanity.

Eccles. i. 2.

TIMATE XXXVIII.

THE
VANITY
OF ALL
EARTHLY THINGS.

Vanity of vanities, faith the preacher, vanity of vanities, all is vanity.
Eccles. i. 2.

E 2   THE

THE VANITY OF ALL EARTHLY THINGS.

THERE are truths which every person allows to be as certain as they are important; and yet, in regard of most men, are as barren and unfruitful as if they deemed them trifles, or doubtful hypotheses. We are not to be surprised at this. Man, corrupted man, is a creature seldom consistent with himself, and whose actions are generally contradictory to his knowledge. Whence does this arise? He hardly stops at common notions, which, because they are common, affect him but little,

little, or even not at all. He loses himself amidst the numberless multitude of the very things to which it belongs. He concerns himself not with the particular relation every truth has with him and his moral situation, as he knows beforehand that such investigations must end in his humiliation, his confusion, his embarrassment, and his disquiet.—Who is there, Sirs, that doubts, (that I may explain what I advance by a familiar example), who is there that doubts for a moment about the vanity of all earthly things? Who does not believe that our lives are uncertain and short; that all the pre-eminences, possessions, and pleasures of the earth, are unsatisfying and transient; and that, at length, the semblances of this world vanish away? But, does the acquiescence that all men give to these truths produce the fruits of virtue and piety they are so naturally adapted to bring forth? Does it, in general, render them humble, and heavenly minded? Does it moderate their attachment and love for that which is vifible and fleeting? Does it teach them to make a true and certain ufe of the advantages which God has given them, and of the ineftimable time he affords them? Does it infpire them with a true zeal for the concerns of futurity, and induce them to prepare for that neverending life, to which they are every hour and every moment approaching? Does it move them to hold fuch a conduct as becomes the citizens of heaven and the candidates for immortal felicity?—No.—The moft woeful experience demonftrates the reverfe. Thefe truths are fufficiently believed; but they are not thought upon with ftedfaftnefs and frequency enough. They are totally loft from our fight too foon. They are fometimes purpofely banifhed from our mind. At leaft, we do not often enough turn our reflections on ourfelves and our conduct. And hence it arifes, that we do not feel their falutary influence.—I conceive it, therefore, to be my duty, Sirs, to admonish you and myself of these truths; and to devote the present moments to the subject of the vanity of all earthly things.

You know who was the author of this just and well-known speech; and when you consider the principal circumstances of his life, it will not be difficult for you to perceive his judgement in this matter must have great weight; as it is grounded on an exact knowledge of earthly things, and a loug experience of their agreeableness, on one side; and on their insufficiency and emptiness on the other.

Were it some gloomy moralist, some anchorite, or misanthropist, who, destitute of all the conveniences of life, from his dismal solitude, surrounded by the shades of death, called out to you, that all was vanity; you would probably vouchsafe no regard

regard to his voice. His testimony would make no impression on you. You would be inclined to complain, that you were to be taught by him, and to take his word in such a matter as this. You might declare him incompetent to pronounce on the value of things, which perhaps he had never seen, had never possessed, had never enjoyed; and which he only reviled, as you might imagine, because he was obliged to forego them. Is not this very often the precipitate and partial judgement you pass on the admonitions of your teachers, and by which you not unfrequently destroy their effect? When we represent to you all that is terrestrial and visible as empty and vain; when we discourse to you of the honours, of the possessions, of the joys of this world, as of things that deserve but small estimation and love; when we maintain that the possession and enjoyment of such things can procure no real happiness to a rational and immortal

immortal creature; when we tell you, that we are here upon earth in a state of exercise and discipline, and this is by no means our home; when we exhort you principally to aspire after heavenly and eternal things, and to provide for futurity; with how many persons do these declarations and admonitions lose all their weight, because they imagine, and that frequently without the slightest foundation, that it is in a manner from constraint, and more from duty than from conviction, that we so judge and so discourse; and that we probably should soon change our language, were we thrown into another way of life, or if we were placed in different, and, according to the general opinion, more fortunate circumstances! I will not now examine the weakness and insufficiency of these evasions and excuses; I will not say, that truth, virtue, and religion, remain for ever; and that they therefore always, as such,

such, deserve our esteem, our obedience, and our submission, let their teachers and defenders conduct themselves as they will. I shall at present only appeal to the expression of the author of our text, against whose testimony no one, not even the corruptest of the worldly-minded, can bring any specious accusation either of ignorance or partiality. It is Solomon who makes his appearance as the teacher of the human race, calling out to deluded mortals, " It is all vanity, it is all vanity!" And who was this Solomon? Was he some unfortunate prince, who met unsurmountable difficulties in every thing he undertook; who was hated of his subjects, who was plagued and persecuted by his neighbours; who, by a long series of afflictions, had lost all heart and taste for every beautiful and charming object of the earth; or who did not know the more refined and nobler pleasures of life? No. He was, as we learn from his history, the wisest and the

hap-

happiest monarch of his times. Beloved of his subjects, feared by his neighbours, respected by remoter nations, he enjoyed a flourishing and uninterrupted prosperity. The most extensive and uncommon knowledge adorned his mind; and his power left him in want of no resource for executing and extending his views, and for satisfying his desires, if they were to be satisfied. The splendor and magnificence of his court, the excess of his treasures, and the wisdom he displayed in his actions and discourses, made his very name revered in foreign lands. With these advantages he possessed whatever can flatter the senses, all that his heart could desire and satiate him with joy in superfluous abundance. To him no kind of pleasure was unknown; and his days were spent in jollity and mirth. Hear how he expresses himself on this: " Whatsoever mine eyes desired I kept not from; I withheld not my heart from any joy." But hear likewise what judgement

ment he passes upon all his pleasures: "And behold all was vanity, and vexation of spirit." This is what he also maintains in other passages, and indeed throughout the whole of his book of moral sentences. Ye who love the world and its pleasures more than your God, who place your highest felicity in the possession and enjoyment of earthly things, and seek your supreme satisfactions in them, what have ye to bring against such a testimony as this? Must it not make the deepest impression upon you? must it not awaken you from your carnal lethargy, and bring you to reflection, when you hear so wise, so powerful, and so fortunate a monarch; when you hear the acutest judge, the most tranquil possessor of every fair and charming thing the earth contains, declare, "that all is vanity; that all is vanity?"

Yet his evidence, strong and incontrovertible as it is, is not the only, is not the firmest

firmest foundation on which the truth of this matter rests. The very nature of the thing, the constant and unvarying experience of all men, and of all ages, our own sentiments, and the testimony of our own hearts, set it beyond all doubt. We need only to turn a glance of observation on the quality of the matters we treat of; we need only compare them together on their different sides; we have only to ask ourselves how far they contribute to make us happy, for acquiring a perfect conviction of the justice of Solomon's assertion, "Riches and honours, the pleasures of sense, wisdom and knowledge, life itself, all is vanity." That is, all these advantages are fleeting and inconstant; they last but a short time; they are not capable of satisfying the human heart, of completing its desires, and of filling it with a real and durable felicity. Let us examine them somewhat more particularly apart.

The greatest riches are vain. I will not here take notice how much labour and toil, how many sleepless nights, how many low and servile actions, how many abnegations of the most innocent pleasures, to acquire a superfluity, it costs the generality of men. I will not remark what a considerable portion of life is spent therein, before they have reached their aim, and how often they lavish their abilities in vain, and how often they fail of the term towards which they ran with the most anxious solicitude. We will allow that they have surmounted all these difficulties, and that they are in actual possession of the greatest treasures. What sort of treasures are they? Are they not, in their very nature, fleeting and inconstant? Are they not treasures, which, as the sapient king observes, often make themselves wings, and quickly leave their possessor? May not a man be deprived of them by a thousand disastrous events, which he is neither able to foresee or prevent? May he not, when he is least thinking of it, be plunged from the height of opulence down to the depths of poverty and indigence? And is he ever perfectly sure that this will not presently happen? And will these treasures follow him into the other world? Must he not at his death forsake them for ever? Can these things satisfy their possessor, be they of long or of short duration? Can they make him really happy? Does not constant experience convince us, that the thirst of gold and silver is always increasing in violence, and that it is never to be allayed?—Or can these possessions assuage our pains? Can they give us health and strength when we lie languishing in disease? Can they heal our spirit when it is wounded, or remove cares and disquietudes from our hearts? Can they restore us the loss of a darling spouse, an only son, or a trusty friend? Can they shield us from the terrors of death? Must they not rather make the

sight

sight of the grave more hideous to us than it is in itself? How true it is, in all these respects, that a man's life consisteth not in the abundance of the things which he possesseth!

But, perhaps, the honour of this world is less vain than riches? Perhaps that may be more adapted to procure us an essential and lasting felicity than they? How egregiously, Sirs, should we err, were we to pay the slightest attention to this supposition! Wherein, then, consists the honour of this world? In the proportionate judgements which other men form of our preeminences, of our endowments and abilities, of our virtues and merits. And on what is this judgement founded? But seldom is it the effect of a mature and impartial consideration, a true knowledge of our character and conduct, an undissembled esteem for the worth and virtues we possess. It is founded in general on the outward appearance we make, which vanishes away on a closer inspection, or upon some fortunate incident, or on mean self-interest, or on treachery and falshood. One will honour us, that we may do honour to him in return. Another will praise our merits, that he may acquire the reputation of being a discerner and a protector of desert. A man will applaud virtue in others, that he may conceal the want of it in himself, and that he may be thought their friend. We are frequently flattered for the sake of gaining our affection, our assistance, our support, or for more effectually doing us hurt. And who are they whose approbation and applause compose what is usually called the renown of the world? They are for the most part men that are destitute of all respectable and praise-worthy qualities themselves; who suffer themselves to be guided by their fancies, their passions, their fears, and their hopes; with whom prejudice and caprice do the office

of

of principles; who trust to every ambiguous or doubtful report, and never afford it their investigation; who frequently know not what is either truly great, or honourable, or noble; and therefore, according to the expression of the prophet, call light darkness, and darkness light. They are men who generally only pronounce on the generality of actions according to their success, without attending to the motives and the intentions of them; who admire and revere whatever is uncommon, whatever makes noise and parade, but disregard unostentatious virtue, and value not the truly magnanimous actions which the wise and good man performs in the noiseless tenor of his life. What then is more changeable and inconstant than the judgement of mankind? How small a matter is necessary for making you forfeit their favour? How often does it happen that they dislike, reject, depreciate, and condemn, the very things they approved and extolled to the summit of praise but the day before! Is not history full of examples of such persons as have been for some time the darlings of the people, and on a sudden have become the objects of their bitterest hatred and most implacable fury? Shall then the honour and applause of this world, which commonly rests upon so slight a foundation, which is distributed by such partial judges, which is so easily lost and turned into disgrace, which procures us no essential advantage, which ordinarily, on the contrary, poisons our hearts, and renders us insensible to the infinitely more precious approbation of God and our conscience, puffs us up with a ridiculous but guilty pride, which at length must fade and be buried with us in the grave, can it satisfy our spirits, and secure us a real and lasting felicity? Can it be any thing but fancy, folly, and vanity?

And

And must we not pronounce the same of sensual pleasures, which such numbers of deluded mortals take for their greatest comforts? How vain, how fleeting, how instantaneous are they! They elude us the moment we begin to enjoy them; they die, as it were, in their birth; and never answer the expectation of him that pursues them. We look towards them with the greatest desire, we seek them with painful trouble, we promise ourselves the most ravishing joy in their possession, and esteem ourselves happy in the prospect; and no sooner is our desire assuaged than we find ourselves cheated; we awake, and the shadowy vision, that delighted us in our dream, is gone; and our rapture is turned into disgust, aversion, and remorse, after giving place to the deepest confusion, the most pungent sorrow, and the painful stings of conscience. The most exquisite sensual delights, by repeated enjoyment, lose their charms; and the narrow circle of worldly joys is so run through, that no diversification is able to restore their intrinsic defects. Our senses become enfeebled by degrees, our powers exhausted, our passions less active, and what we before deemed the most delightful sensations, become shortly indifferent to us, or even change to a grievous burden. We find ourselves all obliged, sooner or later, to say of laughter, it is mad; and of mirth, what doth it? But can pleasures be so contrived, as to satisfy our soul? Can they yield a sufficiency for our capacious desires which proceed to infinitude? Can we, without purposely deceiving ourselves, seek in them a true, a durable happiness, a happiness suited to our capacities? Ye who follow your inclinations, and lead a sensual life, we appeal to your own experience. Can you deny it, that the pleasures you so eagerly pursue very often deceive you, that they very often border on dissatisfaction, and that it commonly follows

lows them close behind? Can you deny it, that you frequently feel a secret remorse disturbing you in the midst of your delights, and embittering their enjoyment; and that your heart, amidst every thing delicious and charming that this earth affords you, remains empty and unsatisfied? And, if you cannot deny this, you thereby confess that all sensual pleasures are vain, and incapable of procuring a solid felicity to man.

But may not the pleasures of the mind, which their admirers call wisdom and knowledge, be exempt from these defects, may they not be sent to procure us what the others cannot possibly give? No, Sirs. They are likewise vain; *In much wisdom is much grief*, saith the Preacher, *and he that increaseth knowledge, increaseth sorrow*. And indeed, when we consider how much time and toil, how much reflection, how much difficult, and sometimes unpleasant investigation,

tigation, are neceffary to acquire what is called wifdom and knowledge; and how little we obtain by the moft conftant application and the moft ftrenuous efforts, how fhort we fall of our defigns, after the exertion of all our powers; and what a tafk it is to diftinguifh what is important and of ufe to human fociety, difcoveries that tend to its real improvement, from the amazing heap of writings by fuch as are called the wife and learned; when we reflect how many infurmountable difficulties and obftacles, how many enemies and dangers we meet with on the way that leads to truth, how often our underftanding betrays us, obfcured by prejudice, or blinded by paffion; how apt we are to take appearance for reality; how often one fingle ray of light points out to us the vanity of what we have been labouring upon for feveral years, and reprefents the moft ingenious fyftem, which we held to be immoveable, as having no foundation

at

at all but in the flimzy materials of our own imagination; when we confider the weaknefs of our reafon, the shortnefs of our view, and to what narrow limits all our faculties are circumfcribed, how imperfect and infignificant is human knowledge, in comparifon of what we do not, and of what we cannot know, and how obfcure, how vague, how doubtful and incomplete the moft of our conceptions are; when we, in fhort, obferve that the higheft of the human race are moft fenfible of their weaknefs, and acknowledge the deficiency of their penetration in the plaineft terms; that new depths are continually opening before them which they cannot fathom, and that it is infufficient to fatisfy their inordinate defires: I fay, when we ponder upon all this, we cannot deny the vanity of all human wifdom, we are forced to confefs, that it is hidden from the eyes of all living creatures. The thoughts of mortal men are miferable, and all their judgements are uncertain. And how much is the value of this wisdom lessened by its being, like all other things, subject to caducity, and of very short duration? Let the scholar, or the sage, collect ever so much knowledge, and ever so uncommon; let him understand all languages, all the works and monuments of antiquity, the whole compass of antient and modern history, all the experiments mankind have made for explaining the occult operations of nature; all the conjectures that have been formed upon them; let him comprehend all the arts and sciences, as perfectly as they can be understood; we will acknowledge his merits, and not refuse him the honour that is so justly his due; but will he continue to possess this knowledge in the grave? will he take it with him into the other world? Will it then appear to him either so great or so important as he now thinks it to be? Certainly not. He will forget the greatest

part

part of it for ever. He will, at his laſt recollections, bluſh at his childiſh errors, his precipitate judgements, and his raſh deciſions. He will conſider moſt things in a quite other manner, and then, for the firſt time, come out of darkneſs into light. In this reſpect what the Preacher elſewhere ſays is true; " There is no work, nor device, nor knowledge, nor wiſdom, in the grave whither we go."

And how ſoon does this revolution take place with mortals! Our life itſelf is altogether vanity. It laſts but a very ſhort time; and the greateſt part of it glides imperceptibly away, unuſed, and unenjoyed. We are continually advancing to the ſilent grave, and to the endleſs ages of eternity; and before we are aware of it, we ſtand on the verge of our earthly career. We are on no day, at no hour, in no moment, ſecure from death. Neither youth, nor health, nor ſtrength, neither riches,

nor

nor honours, can defend us from this king of terrors. The unconscious child, the blooming youth, the vigorous man, as well as crouched and trembling age, muſt hear and obey his call. But few reach the period of human life; and the greateſt part muſt away before they have taſted the comforts, the advantages, and the pleaſures of it; before they have well begun to live. And how far then is this period from us? Is it perhaps a thouſand years remote? is it a whole century before us? Though it were, yet, compared to eternity, that would be but as the twinkling of an eye. No. "The days of our age are threeſcore years and ten; and though men be ſo ſtrong that they come to fourſcore years, yet is their ſtrength then but labour and ſorrow; ſo ſoon paſſeth it away, and we are gone." Can we then, in any of theſe reſpects, doubt in the ſmalleſt degree of the truth of Solomon's exclamation, "All is vanity; all is vanity?"

But

But it would be a lamentable truth indeed if it were of no service to us. If then we would reap advantage from it, we must give it a constant and practical authority over our life and conduct. It must moderate our esteem and affection for the comforts and pleasures of the world, and make us treat them with a generous contempt. It must induce us to seek our happiness and joy where they are only to be found, and to pursue with all our ardour the possession and enjoyment of those things that are constant and eternal.—And what are these things? God, Sirs, God is eternal. He hath always been, and will for ever be. His mercy is unchangeable: he is the uncreated source of all illumination, all life, and felicity. Whoever is of his acquaintance, of the number of his friends, may promise himself an eternal, an uninterupted felicity. Our spirit is immortal. If it had a beginning, yet it will know no end. It will never discontinue to think, to will, to be happy

happy or unhappy. It will live when our body is crumbled in the grave, and reduced to duft and afhes. Truth and virtue are eternal: no change of time can ruin them. They will furvive the deftruction of the world. They will be in the new heaven, and on the new earth, what they are at prefent. They will then be the perfection and happinefs of all rational creatures. Thefe are things that merit all our attention, and all our cares. Thefe muft therefore be the object of all our defires, our views, and toils. When we place ourfelves in the way of repentance, of faith, and fanctification, we affure ourfelves of the favour and complacency of the Moft High.; when we make the redemption and the falvation of our immortal fpirit our principal concern; when we feek in earneft the kingdom of God and his righteoufnefs; when we endeavour to advance in the knowledge of revealed truth, and in the practice of the chriftian virtues, and to become rich in good

good works; then our happiness rests upon a sure foundation; then we walk the way that leads to true enjoyment, to solid and eternal bliss; then may we be tranquil amid the vicissitudes of all earthly things, and behold with indifferent eyes their emptiness and vanity. Then, let the heavens pass away, and the earth be removed, let the elements be melted with fervent heat, and every work of man be destroyed; we shall still remain; we shall stand upon the ruins of a decomposed world, and our hopes will never be put to confusion.

OF

THE MORAL CHARACTER

OF

JESUS CHRIST.

Let this mind be in you which was alſo in Chriſt Jeſus.

        Philipp. ii. 5.

OF

THE MORAL CHARACTER

OF

JESUS CHRIST.

THE character and conduct of Jesus Christ is proposed to us in scripture as a model for our own, and we are under the strongest obligations to frame our own upon it. This is a proposition which the writers of the New Testament frequently hold out to us, repeat on all occasions, and most earnestly inculcate upon us. Certainly it must be of great importance; it must be closely connected with the design of Christianity; it must form an essential part of it. No doubt but it is. It were a solecism in terms to say we are christians, and not follow the example of the founder of christianity, and not use all diligence to express it in our whole deportment. Indeed he was so pre-eminent over whatever we know of the human race, that it is more than probable we must fall short, in various degrees, of his sublime example. He was the Son of God: he was an extraordinary teacher: he was endued with superior gifts. He performed many actions which we cannot imitate; as neither our abilities, nor the regards in which we stand towards God and man, nor our vocations, nor the circumstances in which we are placed, are adapted to them. But the virtuous, the pious, the beneficent, and magnanimous sentiment which is the principle of all the discourses and actions of Jesus, the pure and generous views he had therein; the ardour, fidelity, and resolution with which he executed the will of his heavenly Father, and the business that was given him to do; the meekness,

the

the patience, the benevolence he displayed in his whole behaviour: these are what we are to propose for our pattern in every part of our conduct. In these particulars we may, and must have, that mind in us which was also in him; and so walk as he also walked.

I feel the difficulty, Sirs, I feel how hard it is to delineate the great, the exalted, the amiable character of Jesus, and to place it in its proper light. And, if I were ever desirous of greater abilities and talents, of a nicer sensibility to moral excellency, it is at this moment when I am venturing on such an astonishing object. Every thing that is great, and beautiful, and good, unite themselves together in it. It is a portrait without a fault; a virtue without defect; an entire life composed of unspotted integrity, of untarnished honour, of unremitted beneficence in mind and heart.

Jesus was perfectly free from all faults and failings. No sin, no infirmity, no mean views, no low desires, no negligence or inactivity in goodness, ever once obscured the lustre of his resplendent merit. He was holy, harmless, and undefiled. He did no sin, neither was guile found in his mouth. He could, with the greatest unreserve, appeal to the testimony of his enemies; and say to them, as he did, "Which of you convinceth me of sin?" Peruse the history that is transmitted to us of his life; and you will not find, either in his speech or his actions, any the slightest indication of pride, or ambition, or hatred, or revenge, or sensuality, or any other baleful passion; but you will always meet with the plainest demonstrations of the virtue that is in opposition to every fault.

How pure, how exalted, how constant and active was the piety of our beloved Lord! The profoundest veneration, and
the

the tenderest love towards God, his heavenly Father, filled and employed all the faculties of his soul. They animated and directed the whole of his conduct. Solitary and familiar converse with this Sovereign Being was the nourishment and invigoration of his spirit. He accustomed himself, not only to attend carefully and regularly the public worship; he observed not only all the established usages of it, but he walked always as in the presence of God. His thoughts and his heart were incessantly directed to him. He was constantly occupied in meditation and secret prayer; and neither the wearisome labours of the day, nor the terrors of darkness, could hinder him from passing whole nights in devotion.

His obedience towards God, his heavenly Father, was as voluntary as it was constant and unchangeable. Behold I come, says he, to do thy will, O God! He reckoned it his meat and his drink to do the will of him that sent him, and to finish his work. It was his pleasure, his delight, to fulfill the designs of divine compassion, and to accomplish the salvation of men; and this he infinitely preferred to all sensible pleasures and earthly joys.—His will was to bring the will of his heavenly Father to perfection, and was in complete submission to it. He adored the divine providence in all its ways; he reverenced the wisdom of the Most High in every dispensation it had made for the deliverance and the salvation of sinners: he rejoiced therein, and reposed entirely on the good pleasure of his Father. "Yes, Father," was he heard to say on various occasions, "Yes, Father; for so it seemeth good in thy sight." Even in the last and dreadfulest scene of his life, when he saw nothing but opprobrium and shame, nothing but grief and pain before him; when he was surrounded by the terrors of death; even then he remained stedfast to the purpose of perfecting the will of God. He over-

overcame the horrors the sight of these agonies occasions to human nature, and said, with the most absolute submission, "Father, if it be possible, let this cup pass from me;—nevertheless, not as I will, but as thou wilt."

What a pure, what an active zeal for the honour of the Most High discovered itself in all his discourses and actions! How exact, how careful, how indefatigable was he in the performance of the weighty business he had to do! How worthily did he fill up the character he bore! No slander, no malice of his enemies, could once turn him aside from his course, or impede him in fulfilling the duties of his office in their largest extent, and with the most punctual precision. No obstacles, no difficulties, were able to deter him from it, no opposition to dishearten or dismay him. His business was to seek the lost, and to preach the gospel to the poor. He was to heal the sick, and

to

to support the weak. And this he did at all times and in all circumstances, though the Pharisees and Theologues insulted him thereupon, and called him the companion of publicans and sinners. Never did he lose the object of his mission from his view. Never did he neglect an opportunity to call the attention of his hearers to it, and of instructing them in the purpose of his appearance in the world. If he heal the sick, he requires them to have confidence in him as a condition of their recovery, as all the surprising actions he performed were directed to this end, to enforce his doctrine on mankind, and to convince them that what he said and did was with authority and power. Do they bring him word: " Behold thy mother and thy brethren stand without, desiring to speak with thee;" he immediately replies, " Whosoever shall do the will of my Father which is in heaven, the same is my brother, and sister, and mother." Do they give him the account of the
unhappy

unhappy people whose blood Pilate had mingled with their sacrifices; he makes no observation upon it, but turns it to a weighty admonition to his hearers: "Suppose ye that these Galileans were sinners above all the Galileans, because they suffered such things? I tell you, Nay: but, except ye repent, ye shall all likewise perish." Do they ask him, from a criminal or a useless curiosity, " Lord, are there few that be saved?" He gives them no direct reply, but endeavours to call the attention of those that ask him, as well as those who stand by, to more essential concerns: "Strive to enter in at the strait gate: for many, I say unto you, will seek to enter in, and shall not be able." Thus had Christ his high vocation constantly before his eyes; and he was concerned about nothing but the glory of his Father, and the work he had given him to do.

But, if the piety of our Saviour was so pure, so lofty, and so active, it must necessarily

sarily have produced the noblest fruits in his dispositions and deportment towards mankind. And here, Sirs, the amiable character of Jesus displays itself in the most radiant colours. The most sincere, the most ardent, the most unconquerable benevolence had full possession of his soul: " Mercy is better than sacrifice. It is more blessed to give than to receive." These were the grand principles on which he built the whole of his conduct; and he testified the importance of them on all occasions, both to his friends and his foes. The view of the miserable condition of his countrymen, in regard to their knowledge, their religion, and their morals, excited his feelings to the tenderest compassion. The burdens their teachers imposed on them, the wretched instruction they gave them, the disordered state of their public affairs at that period, and the far greater calamities he saw approaching, touched him uncommonly near, they filled his whole heart with emotion, they

they drew tears from his eyes. When he saw the multitudes, says Matthew, he was moved with compassion on them, because they fainted, and were scattered abroad, as sheep having no shepherd. "Come unto me," says he therefore to them, " all ye that labour and are heavy laden, and I will give you rest." Even in regard to their corporeal wants he was by no means indifferent or insensible. "I have compassion on the multitude," says he to his disciples, " because they continue with me now three days, and have nothing to eat; and I will not send them away fasting, left they faint in the way."— Does Christ pronounce a woe upon Chorazin and Bethsaida; it is only as a warning to the inhabitants of those towns, to call them to reflection and amendment, to deplore their unhappy condition, and to shew that he takes a compassionate concern in their welfare. Does he speak of the righteous punishment that is shortly to overtake Jerusalem and its citizens; does he represent

sent to them their obstinate opposition to all the pains he takes for their salvation; then is he heard to say with inward tenderness and sorrow, "O Jerusalem, Jerusalem, how often would I have gathered thy children together even as a hen gathereth her chickens under her wings;" how often have I offered you grace and deliverance, how often have I invited you to become subjects of my kingdom, and to take part in the benefits of it; " and ye would not!" While describing the calamities he foresaw advancing towards this famous but in the highest degree corrupted city, he displays the most animated compassion towards it. He laments that their present circumstances would prevent their escaping them by a hasty flight. He even wishes them who still adhered to the Jewish ceremonies, and consequently were enemies to his doctrine, not only no harm, but he gives them the most wholesome advice: " Pray ye that your flight be not in the winter, neither on the sabbath-day." Nay, even when he was

bearing

bearing the burden of the crofs; when he was going to meet the moft ignominious death; when he had the greateft caufe to complain of the inhuman procedures of his brethren; even then thefe tender and compaffionate fentiments were predominant in his heart: " Weep not for me," faid he to them that were affected by the lamentable fituation he was in; " but weep for yourfelves and for your children." And who muft but admire the greatnefs of his love; who is not forced into aftonifhment at the energy of it, when he hears the crucified Jefus, in the midft of the moft cruel torments, fay to the Moft High, " Father, forgive them; they know not what they do!"

But perhaps the philanthropy of our Redeemer was barren and dead? Perhaps it confifted barely in good difpofitions, in tender words, and pious wifhes? No. It appeared in a univerfal, in the moft liberal, and the moft unwearied beneficence.

neficence. "He went about, doing good," is the abbreviated history of his whole life. Helping the miserable, healing the sick, comforting such as sat in the shades of sorrow, instructing the ignorant, reforming the wicked, promoting the temporal and eternal felicity of mankind; this was his principal, his peculiar employment. Never did he refuse his assistance to any that applied to him for help: never did he waste a moment in hesitation about granting whatever he was asked for, unless it were bad or unseemly in itself. Does an afflicted father come and beg his succours from a dying daughter; it immediately follows, "And Jesus rose up and went with him." Does a humane and compassionate master address him to heal his slave; his answer is, "I will come and heal him." Do they bring little children to him, that he may lay his hand upon them, and give them his blessing; He says to his disciples, who testified their displeasure thereat, "Suffer the little children to come unto me, and forbid them not, for of such is the kingdom of God." The kingdom of God confifts of fimple hearts like theirs. And he embraced and bleffed them. Inftead of terrifying the timid, or rejecting the feeble in mind, Jefus, like a tender father, exhorts them to courage, and fills them with affurance. "Be of good cheer," fays he to the poor afflicted creature, who, from modefty, would not venture publickly to lay her fituation before him ; " Be of good cheer, O daughter, thy confidence in me hath made thee whole; get thee in comfort home." " Fear not," faid he to an elder of the fynagogue, to whom they brought the difmal tidings of his daughter's death ; " truft only to me, and thy daughter will be well."

Even to the moft unworthy was Jefus beneficent and kind. He had an affection for his very enemies, and did them more good,

good, than we can sometimes afford to our friends. He knew from the first, says his historian John, who it was that should betray him. And yet he did not strike out this base betrayer from the number of his Disciples. And yet he vouchsafed him, for several years, his instruction, his attentions, his intercourse, his friendship. And yet he honoured him with the important commission of announcing the kingdom of God, as well as his trusty dependants, and imparted to him, no less than to them, the gift of shewing signs in his name. How ought this magnanimous conduct of Jesus to have affected the heart of the ungrateful Disciple, and have inspired him with more virtuous, and more noble dispositions, if he had been capable of them! Yet, in the evening, when he designed to execute his horrid purpose, our affectionate Lord endeavoured to make him privately feel his reproof, and bring him to a better mind.

mind. "Woe to the man, how grievously I pity the man, by whom the son of man is betrayed." And with what wonderful meekness does our Master accost him when he comes to deliver him into the hands of his enemies! "Friend," says he to him, "wherefore art thou come? Dost thou betray the son of man with a kiss!"—Nay, what an extraordinary proof of his magnanimous, his unconquerable love, that he should devote his life to deliver us from sins, and so to sacrifice himself for our salvation! His beneficent affection, his unalterable tenderness, triumphed over opprobrium and pain, it stood unchanged and undismayed in the valley of the shadow of death, and mounted thereby to the summit of perfection.

Uncircumscribed, and universal, and unremitted as his philanthropy and lovingkindness to the human race, so tender and constant was his friendship.—" Lazarus, our friend," says he, " is asleep; I go to awaken him." And how full of affection was his gentle heart, when he came up to the grave of his friend! This sight, and the lively idea of human misery that it suggested, drew tears from his manly eyes. He wept; and the standers-by exclaimed, " See how much he loved him!"—With what a firm and generous friendship did he unite himself to his Disciples! A friendship which all their failings, all their infirmities, could neither dissolve nor diminish. Having once loved any, he loved them to the very last. How pungently was his soul afflicted on thinking that one of the twelve, one of so small a number, whom he had hitherto honoured with his confidence, should betray him, by discovering to his persecutors the place of his nightly solitude! How great was his solicitude for the welfare of his friends in that remarkable event! " If ye seek me," said he to those who were come to take him,

him, "then let thefe go their way." And what a ftrong inftance of the moft exalted friendfhip did he give but a few hours before his fufferings! Forgetful, as it were, of himfelf, and the dreadful forrows that now furrounded him;—unmindful of the ignominious and painful death that now awaited him, that he might comfort, and ftrengthen, and prepare, and preferve them againft the terror of his crucifixion. "Let not your hearts be troubled," he faith to them, "you believe in God, believe alfo in me. Have confidence in God, have confidence alfo in me. Ye now have forrow; but I will fee you again, and your heart fhall rejoice, and your joy no man taketh from you. Peace I leave with you; my peace I give unto you; not as the world giveth give I unto you. Let not your heart be troubled, neither let it be afraid."—Only read, Sirs, yourfelves the laft difcourfes of our poor, defpifed, infulted Jefus, which John has left us. I think you will not read them without tears. I am sure you cannot without emotion, if your hearts are capable of generous and friendly feelings.

But we muſt go farther, to remark ſomething of the other amiable qualities and conſpicuous virtues of our great leader; but, as the magnitude and excellency of the object will not allow us to trace a perfect likeneſs of it, we muſt therefore be contented with detached and feeble ſtrokes.

How kind, how friendly, and how affable was Jeſus in his ſocial manners! The dignified gravity he diſplayed in all his actions and diſcourſes, ſo confiſtent with his character, hindered him not from being companionable and pleaſant. He ſhunned not human ſociety; he condemned not the indifferent cuſtoms he found in faſhion therein; he did not deny himſelf its innocent pleaſures. On the contrary,
he

he sometimes participated in them; he honoured with his presence the nuptials of his kinsman in Galilee. He aimed at nothing particular in his daily converse; but conformed on these occasions to the established usages whenever they were neither sinful nor superstitious. " I am come eating and drinking," says he; I eat and drink as other men do, that is, without distinguishing himself from them by an austere and extraordinary temperance.

How wonderful were both his gentleness and complacency towards his Disciples, as well as towards the Jews of his time! They, no less than these, were imbued with the grossest and most servile prejudices in matters of religion; and all his remonstrances and apposite representations were not only incapable of removing, but insufficient to weaken those prejudices in any degree. They, as well as these, had such rude conceptions, so little perspicacity and observation, that they often mistook his plainest propositions, and could not comprehend his easiest apologues. Was he therefore fatigued with instructing and explaining? Did he deliver himself up to the impatience and dejection which any other teacher, in similar circumstances, would have felt and sunk under? No. He bore with patience their infirmities and failings. He even did not always rebuke wickedness, when that rebuke would have been productive of irritation rather than amendment or advantage. He thought it better to redouble his zeal in instructing; he accordingly repeats his doctrines, one while delivering them in this manner, and then in another, to adapt them to the capacities of his hearers. And when, notwithstanding, his scholars did not yet comprehend what he meant; when they still, after all he had done, and all he had said, entertained a reprehensible distrust of his pretensions; he shewed that he had more com-

compaffion for their miftakes than anger or difpleafure at their inconfiderateneſs and levity. "O ye of little faith!" faid he on one of thefe occafions, "why reafon ye among yourfelves, becaufe ye have brought no bread? Do ye not yet underftand, neither remember the five loaves of the five thoufand, and how many bafkets ye took up?"

What a generous and noble impartiality he exhibited in his judgements on all occafions! He efteemed, he applauded integrity and virtue wherever he found them. Very far from condemning all fuch as were not in communion with the Jewifh church, very far from pronouncing that all their virtues were but fplendid fins, we hear him publickly admiring the pious difpofitions of a heathen officer, and propofing him as a pattern to others. "I have not found," fays he, "fo great faith, no not in Ifrael." "O woman!" (thus he addreffes dreſſes the Canaanite, who, with perſevering conſtancy, implores him to relieve her daughter) " great is thy faith : be it unto thee even as thou wilt."' Was that young man who aſked him, " Good maſter, what ſhall I do, that I may inherit eternal life;" was he ſtill far ſhort of perfection; had he yet ſuch failings as rendered him unfit to be a follower of Chriſt, and improper for the apoſtolical office ; yet it is ſaid, Jeſus, beholding him, loved him; he was wellpleaſed at the high veneration he had for the divine law, at his deſire to become happy; and he did not reject theſe good qualities, though they were not ſufficient to happineſs.

What a diſintereſted ſincerity and openneſs of heart ſhone forth in all the actions and diſcourſes of this Son of God? Does he endeavour to conceal or extenuate the dangers that awaited his Diſciples, though he found them ſtill ſo weak in faith, ſo deeply

deeply imbued with numberless prejudices, and so totally destitute of courage and fortitude? Does he endeavour to attach them to him by cherishing their false but specious hopes of earthly enjoyments? No. He saith to them expressly: "I send you forth as sheep among wolves. You will be brought before governors and kings for my sake; you shall be hated of all men men for my name's sake. And as for me; the son of man must suffer many things, and be rejected of the elders and chief priests, and scribes, and be slain." Or, does he strive to bring over to him wholly such as had some esteem for him, who were not altogether alienated from him, at least by tacitly upholding them in their erroneous notions of his kingdom, and by putting a gloss upon the hardships that were the unavoidable consequences of becoming a follower of him? Nothing of all this. He tells them plainly; "If any man will come after me, let him deny himself,

himself, and take up his cross, and follow me:" that is, He that will follow me, must renounce all worldly pleasures, and be ready to tread the thorny path which I pursue. " Foxes have holes, and birds of the air have nests, but the son of man hath not where to lay his head. Whosoever he be of you, that forsaketh not all that he hath, he cannot be my Disciple."

But, though his sincerity was so great; yet his prudence and circumspection were no less conspicuous. How often did he escape from the malice of his enemies; how often would they have laid hands on him; how often would they have put him in prison; how often did they attempt to stone him; so often did he defeat their aim! How many captious questions did they propose to him, and how dextrously did he escape their wiles! He used the means true prudence prescribes on such occasions. He frequently withdrew himself from his opponents, he retired from their fury, he betook himself for a length of time into a solitary region, and forbad any to speak of the good he did, left that should irritate the spirit of persecution in his wicked foes against him; that they might not deprive him, before the time, of the power of doing good, and of preaching the kingdom of God. How careful was he to prevent whatever might incite the populace to tumult, or to any violent enterprise! So soon as he observed, that, astonished at his actions, they were desirous of making him their king, he went and concealed himself among the mountains. And what a super-eminent wisdom did he shew in the answers he gave to the insiduous questions of the Theologues and Pharisees, who frequently attacked him in the design of taking him by surprise, and of leading him to furnish them with an occasion to make him hated by the people, or guilty before the procurator of Rome!—At the same time,

time, it was no worldly wifdom he put in practice, no guilty craft, no mean cunning, for palliating the vices and failings of men, that he might gain or preferve their friendfhip. Whenever the work of God, the promoting of truth and virtue, was in queftion, then our leader and king difcovered the livelieft ardour, though he knew beforehand that he fhould thereby procure the hatred and malice of the mightieft and foremoft of the nation. Read the xxiiid chapter of Matthew, and admire the heavenly zeal, the majeftic gravity, the heroic conftancy, with which he warns the deluded people of the pretended fanctity of their fuperiors; and, taking from them the mafk of hypocrify and feigned devotion, overwhelms them with fhame and confufion.

But, if his zeal on fuch occafions were juft and laudable, fo alfo in the higheft degree refpectable were the gentlenefs and patience

patience he displayed on other occasions, that related, not so much to the honour of God his father, as to his own person and his own concerns. His whole life was a continued exercise of this most excellent virtue. Was he traduced by his enemies, and loaded with the vilest abuse; was he withstood by them in the most opprobious manner; did they take up stones to throw at him? He never returned evil for evil, or reproach for reproach; but met their fury with a sedate and sublime tranquillity; and opposed their unjust accusations by rational principles and solid replies. Would the disciples, from too quick a sensibility at a slight offence, have him call fire from heaven to destroy the Samaritanes? As a reprehension for their vehemence, he earnestly says to them, " Ye know not what manner of spirit ye are of. For the son of man is not come to destroy mens lives, but to save them." Do the disciples shew so much indifference and insensibility at the

very

very time when his whole heart was full of grief and affliction, and when he had most need of their comfort and support, and notwithstanding his repeated admonitions to watchfulness, as to suffer themselves to be overcome by sleep? He reproves them indeed for their inattention, but at the same time excuses it himself; and his very reproof is without anger, and only proceeds from friendship and compassion. " What, could ye not watch with me one hour! The spirit indeed is willing, but the flesh is weak." Your bodies are oppressed by fatigue. Is he at length unjustly accused and condemned? Is he, the greatest benefactor to his brethren, most shamefully insulted by them, derided, crucified, and killed? Is he to be suspended, as a transgressor, between two malefactors, on the accursed tree, and be a mark for the general scorn and the most cruel sport? He preserves his spirit in a perfect calm, and free from all the disorder

order of passion. No angry, no malicious, no vindictive expression, proceeds from his mouth; he prays for the barbarous instruments of his unmerited sufferings; he comforts a sincere, though late repenting sinner; he provides for his deserted mother, and for the disciple who had always been his favourite; and then surrenders his spirit, full of confidence and fortitude, into the hands of his heavenly Father.

All these virtues, Sirs, all these merits were clad in the robe of meekness, and thence acquired additional splendor. Our Saviour was not proud of these eminent qualities which elevated him so far above all mortal beings. He did not boast of that superiority which his close imitation of the Most High procured him, insomuch as to render him the chief among ten thousand of his sons, to make him his beloved, and to unite him in the most intimate connection with him. Having these pre-eminences, he laid them all aside, and took upon him the office of a minister. He concealed the great superiority his goodness gave him, and never made use of it, but when the nature of his office, and the design of his mission, demanded it of him. He sought not his own glory, but the glory of him that sent him. He ascribed those wonderful acts he performed, not so much to himself, as to his heavenly Father, from whose providential spirit he received such gifts.—And what an affecting instance of his humility did he give but a short time before his sufferings, by washing the feet of his disciples, and by submitting himself to such services as are only becoming to the meanest domestics!

These, Sirs, are the principal features in the venerable and amiable character of our Saviour Jesus. This is the charming example of goodness and virtue he has left us; and to which he has so forcibly enjoined

joined us to conform. I am perfectly senfible, that what I have prefented to you is far, very far from doing juftice to the excellency of its original; and I am inclined to believe, that it is not poffible for creatures fo feeble, fo frail, and fo corrupted, as we are, to arrive at its complete refemblance. Can we, however, contemplate this picture, all imperfect as it is, without aftonifhment and gentle tranfports? Can we contemplate it without having the higheft veneration for Jefus and his facred religion? without being charmed with the piety and virtue that appears in every part of it? without feeling a frefh zeal to act up to the bright example with all poffible firmnefs and perfeverance? Unhappy they who can confider the moral goodnefs and integrity of fuch a pattern without emotion; or without being infpired with the moft ferious and folemn defires of becoming like it! Such infenfible, fuch groveling fouls, muft be loft to every beautiful, good, and every generous sentiment; they must be unfit for virtue, unfit for religion, and unfit for heaven! Yes, Sirs, if we would be the disciples of Jesus, if we would be happy, we must thus be affected by the example of our Lord. It must by degrees destroy in us all the seeds of inordinate desires; it must produce and strengthen in us every good, every lovely, and every generous inclination; it must inspire us with a well-conducted ardour in the beneficent actions which are well-pleasing in the sight of God. To this end, we must keep this example constantly before our eyes, frequently examine ourselves by it, and make it the pattern of our whole behaviour. We must be like-minded with Jesus, and so walk even as he walked. Oh happy we, if we sincerely do so, and persevere in it even unto death! He will then own us for his children and successors; and as such we shall live with him in the other world for ever.

ESTI-

ESTIMATE XL.

OF THE
IMITATION
OF THE
EXAMPLE
OF
JESUS.

Leaving us an example, that ye should follow his steps.   1 Pet. ii. 21.

ESTIMATE

OF THE

IMITATION

OF THE

EXAMPLE

OF

JESUS.

⸺⸺is an example, that ye should follow his steps. 1 Pet. ii.

OF THE IMITATION OF THE EXAMPLE OF JESUS.

WE have already observed that Jesus performed many things wherein we cannot attempt to imitate him. He was placed in many situations and circumstances, as the Son of God, as an extraordinary teacher, as the Redeemer of men, in which we can never come near him. As such, he possessed prerogatives and powers, which are far superior to ours.

He could and might do such works as we neither can nor may. But it is not so much the particular actions of our Saviour, as the way and manner in which he performed them; it is his disposition of mind, and his whole character, which we are to propose for our example. We are to dispose our conduct by the same rules of righteousness, of philanthropy, and generosity; we are to have the same pure and noble views to the honour of the Most High, and to the promotion of universal good; the same spirit of meekness, of gentleness, of patience, of reconciliation, that animated Christ, must animate us also. We are to practise the virtues he practised, though we cannot in all particular cases give the same or so accurate a demonstration of them. Every one of us must strive to fulfill the duties of his calling, and the end of his existence, with the same fidelity with which Christ accomplished the design of his mission upon earth. We must, like him, use all our faculties

faculties in conformity to the will of God, and earnestly lay hold on all occasions for doing good, and for rendering ourselves useful to others, though these faculties be very various, or though they be seldom or never totally alike. Like our Saviour, we must undergo all the trials which God lays upon us, all the sufferings he sends us, with stedfast patience, and meek submission to his will, though these trials and these sufferings be, neither in their nature and frame, nor in respect of their intention, exactly like those our Redeemer underwent. This is to imitate the example of our Lord. And thus even his very actions that were extraordinary, and superior to our abilities, serve us for instruction and example. However various then and great were the prerogatives which he possessed; however different his station and calling from ours; yet, this notwithstanding, his life can and must be the pattern and rule of ours. The condition of a menial

nial servant is doubtless very much inferior to the station of his master; we may, nevertheless, with the greatest propriety exhort him to imitate the example of his prudent and beneficent master. Not that he can give the very same proofs of prudence, of beneficence, and of love; but as he may display the same prudent, affectionate, and beneficent dispositions that are adapted to his condition. The case is the same in regard to the example of our venerable and amiable Redeemer. A few particular exemplifications will set this matter in the clearest light.

Christ came into the world to seek the lost, and to render them happy. He came to announce the will of God to men, to deliver and redeem them from their aberrations, and to conduct them to the supreme felicity; and to this purpose he devoted his whole life. We cannot certainly do exactly the same. We are not called
to

to the paſtoral office, much leſs can we promote the ſalvation of men to the very ſame degree as he did. But does it thence follow that we can contribute nothing to that end? or, that we may be quite indifferent to the ſalvation of our brethren? May we not, on one hand, do harm to our familiars by our imprudent and ſinful behaviour, ſeduce them into wickedneſs, or ſtrengthen them in it? May we not, on the other hand, edify them by our advice, by our example, and by our affectionate ſuggeſtions, admonitions, and exhortations, and incite them to goodneſs? May we not, by our conduct, render religion and chriſtianity either contemptible or reſpectable? and is it not incumbent upon us to avoid the one and to do the other? Have we not relations, friends, and acquaintances, for whoſe ſpiritual and everlaſting welfare we are particularly bound to provide? Can we not then, and muſt we not imitate our Saviour in this reſpect, ſo as to promote,

mote, each of us, according to his circumstances and abilities, the salvation of our brethren, and to contribute and strive all possible ways thereto, and to prosecute these endeavours with an upright intention and a willing heart, and to allow no difficulties to deter us from them?

Christ also humbled himself. He submitted to undergo all the hardships and miseries of life; nay, and voluntarily suffered a painful and ignominious death, and thereby afforded the most astonishing proofs of meekness and self-denial, and of obedience to God, his heavenly Father. It is is certainly impossible for us to give such severe demonstrations of these virtues, since our situations and circumstances are totally different; and therefore we are not called to do so. Nevertheless, we can and must endeavour to imitate also in this respect the Captain of our salvation. And we effectually do so when we testify meekness

ness and modesty in all our words and works, and never boast of our acquirements, or exalt ourselves upon them; when we prefer to become well-pleasing in the sight of God, before all the satisfactions and delights of the world, willingly undergo whatever he inflicts upon us, and never murmur at it; in short, when we are ready and firmly resolved rather to forego all things, and even to forsake whatever is most agreeable and delightful here on earth, than to neglect the commands of God, and to act against our duty.

Our Redeemer travelled about from one place to another, and every where did good. He restored the dumb to their speech, he gave sight to the blind, health to the sick, life to the dead, and reduced the insane to reason. All his time and all his powers were devoted to further the spiritual and temporal welfare of mankind, and

and his generous and helpful love was manifested every day and every hour, as it were, of his public ministry by new proofs and effects. Now, it is indeed utterly impossible for us to perform the same acts of beneficence which he performed; it is impossible for us to afford the same assistance to our brethren, to administer to them the same relief as he did; but we can and must have, like him, a sincere, a constant, and effective desire to do good. Like him, we can and must endeavour at becoming as useful to others, and to afford them as much and as important services as our capacities admit. We can and must, like him, make the sacrifice of our personal advantage to the general good, and promote our neighbour's real happiness to the utmost of our power. And, when we do so, we imitate the philanthropy, the compassion, and the generosity of our Redeemer, though we evince these virtues according to the diversity of circumstances in which

we

we are placed, and exprefs them by particular inftances and demonftrations. And thus it is in general with all the other portions of the life of Jefus. The imitation does not confift in our leading the fame manner of life as he led, and performing the fame actions as he performed; but in this, that, in every event that befalls us, we fhould be fo minded as he was minded, that we fhould let our fpirit be ruled by his, that we fhould frame our moral character after his, that we fhould make his way of thinking and of acting the pattern of ours. And how manifold and cogent are the reafons we have for fuch an imitation of the excellent example of Jefus!

Firft, this was one of the principal purpofes for which the Redeemer appeared in the world, and paffed a period of his life among mankind. He came not only to inftruct us in the gracious will of the Moft High, and to admonifh us of our duties,
but

but he proposed himself likewise as a perfect and engaging pattern of behaviour towards God, our neighbour, and ourselves. He placed the beauty and the value of virtue in the clearest light by his example, that he might animate us to the love and practice of it. He testified, by his conduct, that it is not impossible, even in a corrupted world, to lead a holy and a godlike life: and that the human nature, by the guidance and support of the spirit of God, is capable of attaining to a very high degree of moral perfection. The express declarations of our Lord himself, as well as the reiterated testimony of his Apostles, leave us no room to doubt that this was the design of his conversation on earth. How clearly the Saviour explains himself hereupon, when he says; "If any man will come after me, let him deny himself, and take up his cross, and follow me! Learn of me, for I am meek and lowly in in heart. I have given you an example,
that

that ye should do as I have done to you. Whosoever will be great among you, shall be your minister: and whosoever of you will be the chiefest, shall be the servant of all. For even the son of man came not to be ministred unto, but to minister, and to give his life a ransom for many. This is my commandment, That ye love one another, as I have loved you." The Apostles of our Lord are ever enforcing the same. Would they incite us to holiness; they give us the precept: As he which hath called you is holy, so be ye holy in all manner of conversation. Would they encourage us to patience and firmness in afflictions; they bid us, Look unto Jesus, the author and finisher of our faith; who, for the joy that was set before him, endured the cross, despising the shame. They remind us, that Christ also suffered for us, leaving us an example that ye should follow his steps. Would they inspire us with humility of mind; they say,

Let this mind be in you, which was also in Christ Jesus; who, being in the form of God, thought it not robbery to be equal with God, or, to glory in being like unto God. Would they incite us to love, to gentleness, to reconcilement; they thus exhort us; Walk in love, as Christ also hath loved us. Bearing one another, and forgiving one another; if any man have a quarrel against any; even as Christ forgave you, so also do ye. If any man have not the spirit of Christ, he is none of his. To be conformed to the image of the son of God. We must live not to ourselves, but to him. We must be pure even as he is pure. He that saith, he abideth in him, ought himself also to walk even as he walked. Because he laid down his life for us; we ought to lay down our lives for the brethren. Thus are we taught in the sayings of Christ and his Apostles. Could they have expressed themselves more plainly and pointedly on this matter than they

they do? After this can we doubt of it for one moment, that it is the purpose and the will of God, and consequently our duty, to follow the example of our Redeemer, and to be constantly approaching nearer to a resemblance with him?

The extraordinary excellence of this example is another consideration, inducing us to the imitation of it. It is a pattern entirely blameless and complete, free from all imperfection and defect, beautiful, consistent, and harmonious in all its parts; which we may safely follow without fear of danger, and by which we may guide ourselves without hesitation in all the events of life. While we tread in the footsteps of Christ, we cannot possibly err; and so surely as we are persuaded that God was satisfied with his conduct, so certainly may we be assured that he likewise will be graciously pleased with ours, if we form it upon that model.—It is also the noblest

noblest and the grandest example that was ever presented to the world. Nothing can more dignify our nature; nothing can procure us more real greatness of mind; nothing can bring us nearer to the divinity, and make us more capable of communion with him, than the being animated with that mind which we admire in our Lord and Saviour Jesus Christ.—It is a universal and most instructive example, adapted to all times and places, to all ranks and orders of men, which may constantly guide and improve us, be we high or low, rich or poor, fortunate or unfortunate. While our Saviour was amongst us, he was in such a variety of circumstances; he stood in such a diversity of relationships; his whole life, during the time of his ministry, was so busy and active, that we may learn from him how we ought to behave towards God and man, what we have to do both in regard to the present and the future, in all the revolutions and events of life.—

life.—It is, in short, an example of the greatest, the most necessary, the most useful and most beneficent virtue; an example of such virtue as in part to appear very difficult, and to be totally out of the reach of the generality of men, and yet is indispensably necessary to our happiness, and to the practice of which we are every day, on one account or other, repeatedly called. But can we think this example so excellent as it actually is, and yet doubt of our obligation to adopt it? Should we not thus contradict ourselves? Should we not deny by our conduct what we confess with our lips? Should we not betray a sordid disposition, and shew a contempt and hatred to virtue, if we hesitated to conform to a rule which we ourselves confess to be faultless, a model which we must admire and revere?

The relationship wherein we stand towards Christ, and the benefits we have received

ceived from him, are a third obligation by which we are bound to the strictest imitation of his life. Even the example of a mean and obscure person, of a stranger to us, one with whom we have no intimate connection or relationship, who has not the smallest power over us, to whom we owe neither obedience nor gratitude, even the example of such an one, if it were good and virtuous, must incite us to imitation. How much more then ought it to do so in a case directly the reverse of this in all relational respects? The pattern of virtue and piety which our religion holds out, is the example of a person invested with the highest prerogatives, and the highest authority, who merits our utmost esteem and affection, with whom we are connected by the most indissoluble bands, to whom we owe the most willing and the most chearful obedience. It is the example of our Lord and master, our chief and Saviour, the founder of our religion, the author

author and finisher of our faith, the judge of the living and the dead, under whose sovereignty we stand, whose subjects we are, on whose sentence our everlasting lot depends. It is the example of our best friend, our generous and valiant deliverer, who humbled himself to the depths of humility, who gave his life for us, for us while we were his enemies, who did and suffered more than any friend ever did and suffered for another. It is the example of our greatest benefactor, without whose benign assistance we should have been totally ignorant, vicious, comfortless, and wretched; to whom we stand indebted for all the light, all the chearfulness, and all the happiness we enjoy. Every virtue we learn of him, he has himself exemplified by the most authentic demonstration. He that commands to do good to others, has himself first done us infinitely more good, than we can ever hope to do. He who requires us to love our enemies, and to forgive

forgive their failings, loved his enemies, and forgave them their trespasses. How much are we bound to the imitation of him by all these obligations! How insensible, how ungrateful, how despicable must we be if all this cannot move us to it! Certainly, if it do not, we are utterly unworthy of being called the Disciples of Jesus; we deprive ourselves of all the advantages and happiness that are promised us under that distinction.

We have, fourthly, the same cause to lead a pious, a holy, a godly, an humble, a heavenly-minded life, as Christ had so to do; and consequently we are, for this reason, bound to follow his example. Or, do we not stand in the same relationship towards the Supreme Being in which Christ himself, considered as a man, was placed? Have we not the very same nature as he had? Ought not the honouring and glorifying of God to be the ultimate end of our

our whole behaviour, and his will the only and unalterable director of it? Are we not juſt as much ſtrangers and pilgrims here on earth, as our Lord and Saviour was? What is there to induce us to love the world and the things of it more, and more highly prize them, than him? Are riches, honours, and pleaſures more our peculiar and higheſt good than they were his? Can they contribute more to our true and eternal felicity, than they could contribute to his? Are they leſs dangerous to us than they were to him? Is it an eaſier matter for us to conquer our corruption, to perfect our holineſs, and to work out our ſalvation, than it was for him to do the buſineſs the Father had given him to perform? Have we leſs need of piety, leſs zeal and application, leſs ſelf denial, and leſs improvement to that purpoſe than our Saviour had for the accompliſhment of his? Can the humility, the gentleneſs, the patience, which ſat ſo gracefully on Chriſt,

the

the Son of God, and turned so much to his glory, be unbecoming or disgraceful to us, miserable sinners? Can what rendered his character so beautiful and venerable, degrade ours, or militate with our condition? Is it less salutary and needful to us than to him, to be made perfect through trials and sufferings? Are we too great to desire to render ourselves acceptable to the Most High, and to be happy by the same way that Christ obtained the approbation of his heavenly Father, and entered into his glory? But, since we cannot assert this, as every man must allow, without the greatest absurdity, then neither can we deny that we are under the strongest obligations to make the pious, holy, godly, humble, and heavenly-minded life of Jesus the pattern and rule of our own.

Our future destination obliges us, lastly, in like manner, to imitate the example of Christ, and to let that mind be in us, which

which was also in him. We are made for immortality. We are to quit this world, after a short and uncertain abode in it, and then to pass into a better and more perfect state. As Christians, we have the lofty hope, that, after death, we shall go to Christ, our chieftain and Saviour, that we shall be with him for ever, that we shall be closely united with him, and partake of the glory he possesses at the right-hand of God. We are, as the Scripture tells us, heirs of God, and joint-heirs with Christ. We are to live and reign with him. As we here have borne the image of the earthly Adam, so shall we hereafter bear the image of the heavenly. But how can we hereafter bear his likeness, if we have not here done our utmost to resemble him? How can we have fellowship with him, and enjoy his blessed society, if our mind and desires be in opposition to his? How can we share in his authority, if we have not sought it in the way of obedience and fidelity,

delity, of piety and virtue, by which he obtained it, as our Lord and leader? Can we be capable of the holy and godly life he leads in heaven, if we do not ſtudy purity and holineſs here on earth? Or, can we imagine that he will acknowledge us to be his, and as ſuch receive us into his heavenly kingdom, if we ſtand in no other connection with him, and have no farther ſimilitude with him, than that we are called by his name, hold his doctrine to be true, and ſhew him an outward reſpect? What have we, in this caſe, to expect, but that dreadful, but righteous ſentence, "Depart from me, ye workers of wickedneſs; I know you not!"

So many and ſuch ſtrong reaſons have we for following the example of our Redeemer, and for being like-minded with him. And ſo certain it is, that unleſs we do ſo, we neither ſupport the name of
Chriſtians,

Chriftians, nor can be happy. Thefe are doctrines fo effentially inherent to religion and chriftianity, that we cannot refufe ourfelves to them, without at once rejecting all religion and all chriftianity. And yet how little are thefe important doctrines thought of! How flender is the influence they have on our conduct! Do all our words and works teftify, do all the effects of our capacities teftify, that we are the difciples and followers of the holy and righteous, the humble and gentle, the beneficent and divine, the heavenly-minded Jefus? O Chriftians, how far inferior are we ftill to the pattern of virtue and piety fet us by our Lord and Saviour! How little refemblance there is between his way of thinking and acting, and ours! How little conformity between our lives and the fanctity of the doctrine we confefs, or the conduct of the Lord to whom we belong! How cold and unfruitful the love we bear

to Chrift, our good Redeemer, and how imperfect and inconftant the obedience we pay him! May thefe reflections alarm and awaken us! May they fill us with the moft fenfible remorfe and affliction at our negligence and ingratitude! May they excite in us a lively zeal to walk worthy of our vocation, and to difcharge our duties with more carefulnefs and fidelity! So fhall we actually do honour to our Redeemer, who hath fo loved us as to lay down his life for us. So fhall we give him the thankfulnefs that is his due, and which he has fo much right to demand. So fhall we adorn the name of Chriftians; we fhall make him the object of our efteem and reverence; we fhall edify others by our behaviour, and fhine as lights in the midft of the corrupt generation of this world. But fo likewife fhall we arrive at the end of our faith, everlafting happinefs. If we, like Chrift, our leader and head, be dead unto fin, and
alive

alive unto God; if we, like him, overcome the world, and, by perseverance in good works, strive after praise, and honour, and immortality; then shall we also, like him, be exalted to glory. We shall then, like him, be filled with joy and bliss at the right hand of God; we shall find the completion of all our wishes in his blessed society, and in the closest intercourse with him.

The PASTORAL OFFICE.

He gave some—pastors and teachers.
                                Ephesians iv. 11.

ESTIMATE

OF THE

PASTORAL OFFICE.

—pastors and teachers.
Ephesians iv. 11.

OF

The PASTORAL OFFICE.

THE paſtoral office, which is every where introduced into the Chriſtian church, and dates its origin from the times of the apoſtles, is certainly an eſtabliſhment of the greateſt utility; an eſtabliſhment which would inſure to Jeſus and his diſciples one of the foremoſt ranks among the benefactors of the human race, were we only to conſider them as wiſe men, and not as peculiar plenipotentiary ambaſſadors from God to mankind. No where do we find in the antient world, as far as it is known to us, any such teachers of the people; teachers that insult their brethren, without distinction of ranks, of ages, of sexes, or manners, in their obligations towards God and man, in their duties, and the matters that concern their present and their future state; who instruct them at stated times, not far asunder, on the most important subjects; who lead them to consideration and virtue, comfort them in their sorrows, and have in such various ways promoted their contentment and happiness. —But we find priests of idols, and imperious leaders of the people, every where, throughout the antient and modern, the heathenish, or the not-christian world; men who could make use of the ignorance and weaknesses of their fellow-creatures to the confirming of a tyrannical and cruel power, to the extorting of rich presents and hard tributes, or to the attainment of other selfish views, who spread fear and terrors around them, and by all the solemnities of their

their religion and worship promoted neither wisdom nor virtue, but were favourable to superstition and vice.—I am well aware, that even the christian pastorate has been very often and very shamefully misused, and is still misused; that it not always, and not thoroughly, is and effects what it can and may effect and be: and this does not at all surprise me, since it is supplied by men, who are subject, like all others, to mistakes and errors, and are so liable to be imposed upon by the passions. At the same time, it has certainly done an infinite deal of good; still, upon the whole, does much good; and will—as we may assuredly hope—in the course of time effect still far more good. The christian teacher undoubtedly therefore merits esteem, on account of the office he bears, and the usefulness he obtains thereby. But, for rendering this a rational esteem, and for giving it a wholesome influence on our conduct; if we are desirous that it should neither degenerate into superstition, nor by degrees give place to disrespect and contempt; it must be grounded on right notions of it, and on what christian teachers are and ought to be. We must not require and expect more from them, than we can with justice require and expect. And to settle these notions, and to render them more common, is the design of my present undertaking. It is written, in the Epistle to the Ephesians, that Christ appointed or ordained some in his church to be pastors and teachers. These are the very persons whom we at present commonly call preachers; and the purport of their institution we will now study more clearly to understand.

We will investigate the relationship wherein a preacher stands to his flock; or, shew you what the preacher properly is and ought to be in regard to his congregation.

To this end we muſt firſt remove the falſe repreſentations that are made of this relationſhip; and

Then exhibit the true nature of it.

In the firſt place, the preacher is no prieſt in the ſtrict and uſual acceptation of the word, but only in that ſenſe wherein it is uſed by the compilers of our liturgy. He is not a perſon that ſtands in any nearer degree of affinity with God, or has a cloſer and more familiar intercourſe with him than the reſt of his worſhipers; he is not a perſon, who, when we have ſinned, can free us from the merited conſequences of the ſin, by offerings, or rites, or interceſſions, and reconcile us again with our affronted Maker. He may and ought to announce to us favour and life on the part of God, ſet the value of his bounties and bleſſings both in nature and religion in their proper light, and excite us to be glad and
rejoice

rejoice therein; but he cannot difpenfe either the one or the other according to his pleafure. He may and ought to promife us the pardon of our fins and everlafting happinefs, on certain conditions, in the name of God; but he cannot actually confer them. He may and ought to explain and inculcate the divine commandments; but he cannot difcharge any from the obfervance of them. Of his own authority he can neither impofe nor invalidate any vow, any obligation, or any duty. He is, therefore, no fuch manager between God and man, as that he can give a greater value to our acts of worfhip than they would otherwife have; or impart, by certain fanctified words, to the water in baptifm, and to the figns of the body and blood of Jefus in the holy communion, any power or efficacy which they had not before; or, laftly, whofe prayers are more acceptable and effectual with God, than the prayers of any other fincere and upright chriftian.—Jefus Chrift

Chrift is reprefented to us in the writings of the apoftles, and particularly in the writings of the apoftle Paul, as the fole highprieft and mediator between God and man, for tranquillizing mankind, and more efpecially the Jews, on the recent abolition of the prieftly office and the facrifices in ufe, by the introduction of chriftianity, for infpiring them with a filial confidence in God, and for affuring them, in a fenfible manner, adapted to their comprehenfions, of his protection and favour. All notions of peculiar priefts and facrifices, that have been adopted in the chriftian religion and the chriftian worfhip, are fuperftitious; they are in direct oppofition to the fcope and the fpirit of our holy religion, and of this pure and rational worfhip; they miflead us from the God to whom Jefus has opened us a free accefs, and whom he has taught us to regard and to love as our father. They are relics of the feeble Jewifh way of thinking, which the chriftian doctrine

trine by degrees abolished, and of which, among christians, who are no longer children, but should be men in knowledge and in faith, no traces ought now to remain.

The preacher is, secondly, no curate of souls, in the strictest meaning of the word, and as it implies a person on whose pains and behaviour the salvation or the happiness of the rest, if not altogether, yet greatly depends; who can and must contribute as much or still more than themselves to their moral improvement, to their spiritual and eternal welfare; and whose future lot is indissolubly connected with the lot of the souls entrusted to his care. No; every individual must be the curate of his own soul, bear his own guilt, and give an account to God for himself. Every person must fulfill his duty according to the utmost of his power; but none can be security for the consequences, much less fulfill it for another. And what sensible man would take the pastoral office upon him, if he must thereby oblige himself to answer for the conduct of all such as belong to his congregation, or to concern himself for the happiness of each of them in particular, as a father concerns himself for his children, or a domestic tutor for his pupil? If this were to be the case; then must he be thoroughly and intimately acquainted with every person in his parish; they must at all times and in all circumstances so exhibit themselves to him as they really are; they must make him the confidant of their most secret dispositions and sentiments; he must be the witness of their conduct in domestic as well as in civil society; he must have the right and the licence to give them the most determinate precepts on all their concernments; and even if all this were done, which yet is not, and will not be, and cannot be, still it must be an effect of the most audacious temerity for a man to assume to himself the peculiar and sole guidance

ance of so many persons of such various capacities and tempers, and to stand as surety for them in the day of judgement.

No; when you call us, preachers, your curates, you cannot reasonably exact any thing more of us, than that, according to our best insights and to your necessities, we should shew you what you ought to do, and how you are to set about it, for delivering your soul from the captivity of error, of sensuality, of vice, or to caution you against them; for adorning it with wisdom and virtue; for rendering it both in this and in the future world as perfect, as happy, and as agreeable to God, as it is capable of becoming. In this design, with no less seriousness than affection, we are to instruct, to exhort, to admonish, to reprehend, and to intreat; to call your attention to whatever may be in an eminent degree useful or prejudicial to you at all times, and on every alteration of your condition;

dition; and all this for earnestly promoting the cause of truth, of virtue, and your happiness; and never to be weary and disheartened in so doing, though attended by the worst consequences. Thus are we to care for your souls, as we must give an account how we have instructed you, and of the use we have made of the times, the circumstances, and the occasions afforded us for that purpose.

We may also, in a stricter sense, be considered as your curates, if you afford us opportunity and encouragement to make what we here deliver and teach in public more profitable to you by friendly and private conversation, apply it more closely to your station and your present occasions, remind you of your particular duties, failings, and transgressions; to labour with you in maintaining or restoring domestic harmony, or to supply you with stated precepts and means for your proficiency in

knowledge

knowledge and virtue. At the same time, as every one readily perceives, the preacher cannot execute this duty of fraternal admonition and particular incitations to goodness, without the concurrence, or against the will, of his parishioner. Neither is this a duty peculiarly incumbent on him: he possesses it in common with every other christian; only in so much as in particular cases and with certain persons, from the greater respect they have for him, and the greater sagacity they may allow him to possess, he may fulfill it with better success than another.

The mistaken and superstitious idea annexed to the office of a clergyman is in nothing so apparent as in regard to the sick and dying. But too frequently almost the whole hope of the salvation of a man is built on the presence, on the discourse, on the prayer of the curate. How sadly are the assistants concerned, that the sick person

son should die without this preparation or succour! What can we conclude from hence, but that they attribute to the clergyman far greater ability and influence than he actually has? We are by no means disinclined to attend when called to the sick and the dying; and when we can excite or cherish any good, any christian reflections and feelings in them, when we are able to administer any thing to their comfort, or for soothing their passage from this into the future world, we do it with all our heart. But it is absolutely impossible for us, or any other man, at such a time, to make a good man of a bad one, or as it were to open the gates of heaven to a sinner who has been a slave to sin and vice his whole life long, and to set him in safety from the penalties he has to dread. And then the visitation of the sick is a duty not obligatory on us alone, but we have it in common with all other christians. It is their duty mutually to support, to comfort,

fort, and to exhort and encourage each other, and to make fupplications for all men. In the primitive church, in the times of the apoftles and their immediate fucceffors, when it was better feen, or more believed, that the portion of a man after death did not depend on the manner wherein he fpent the laft days or the laft hours of his life, but was to be determined by his predominant difpofitions and the whole of his foregoing behaviour; it was not then peculiar to the office of the teacher to vifit the fick and the dying, but it was the duty of the elders and the prefects of the flock; and in regard to the other fex, it was the duty of the matrons or widows to perform that office. Thefe took charge of the fick and the dying with cordial affection as brothers and fifters, confoled them, prayed with them, provided, if they were poor, for their fupport and nourifhment, tended them, and did them numberlefs perfonal fervices. And thefe are

are undoubtedly the best of offices that can be afforded a person at such times, and which every one may execute according to his means.

A preacher is, thirdly, no man of a different kind or species from other men. He is no divine, so far as this term is used to imply either a man completely perfect, or one elevated above all sensible and terrestrial things. This mistaken notion proceeds from the abuse of the term; or, to speak more properly, the epithet itself is misapplied for the purpose of procuring in the earlier times to the teachers of religion a superiority over other men, and of giving them a greater regard. It was then, and it is at present, not unfrequently understood to imply a man that is absolutely indifferent to every thing sensible, to all visible objects, to whatever chears or saddens others; who despises all such matters; whom neither honour nor disgrace, neither riches

riches nor poverty, neither pain nor pleasure can at all affect; who is constantly employed in religious contemplation and peculiar exercises of devotion; whose thoughts are unremittedly directed to the most important and most exalted objects; in whose sight chearfulness and joy, wit and good humour are horrible transgressions; whose presence is baneful to all pleasure, and whose looks diffuse a sullen gloom on all around. No; such men are we not, nor such ought we to be; and if we either could or should be such, we should be either deserving of contempt or compassion, and in any case be prejudicial to society. No; we are entirely like you in whatever constitutes a man in respect to his infirmity, as well as in respect to his better side; and when any of us excell you in wisdom and virtue, it is from no prerogative of our station, but a personal advantage which any one of you may have over us.

It

It is true, that our station and our office afford, or seem to afford, us some resources for improving in wisdom and virtue which you have not. We employ ourselves frequently, and much oftener, and more continuedly, than you, in reflections on God and his will, on the appointment and the duties of man. But how vigilant must we be over ourselves, how much attention must we necessarily exert, if we would prevent these circumstances, so advantageous in themselves, from becoming detrimental to us! For the very reason that we are obliged to employ ourselves so often, and so often solely in regard to others, in the doctrines of religion, and this even at times when we have no particular incitement thereto and are not disposed to them, for this very reason they may lose much of their force in respect of us. These reflections, by their frequent recurrence, may become so habitual to us, as to make us think that we understand and feel the subjects themselves, though all the while we are only thinking of barren words. Hence it happens, that difficulties and doubts are frequently augmenting in proportion as we advance farther in knowledge; and that, on the other hand, the pleasure attendant on meditation and devotion may lose much of its poignancy by the abundance of enjoyment. What a comfort must it be to the christian merchant, or artizan, or any other who is not a clergyman, when on having conscientiously performed the business of the day, in the evening he recollects his scattered thoughts, and can converse, for a shorter or a longer time, with God, and reflect upon his weightiest obligations! Certainly, the pleasure this occupation procures him, must frequently be far more lively than ours, just as a repast is much better relished by a man who has fasted long, than by one who has been almost all the day sitting at a plentiful table. —Besides, we preachers commonly have

not

not so many opportunities and means for exercising ourselves in wisdom and virtue, and for applying their precepts to the various occurrences of common life, as he who stands in more diversified connections with other men, who has such various affairs to mind, such various duties to fulfill, and so many dealings to manage with persons of such different opinions and manners; and likewise in this respect may a well-informed, honest christian, who is no clergyman, easily excell us in wisdom and virtue.

Moreover, we have no other duties and obligations, that are not also incumbent on you. What is true, and right, and good, that same is true, and right, and good, for you, and for us, and for all mankind. Whatever is false, and wrong, and bad, is equally so both to you and to us. What is allowable for you to do, is allowable for us. What God forbids us in his word or by the light of reason, he forbids the same to you. We have all the same law. We must all walk the very same way to praise, to honour, to immortality. If we must give an account how we have discharged our clerical office, so must you likewise render account how you have fulfilled your civil offices, how you have pursued your calling as a merchant, as a manufacturer, as a workman, how you have maintained your post as a master, as a guardian, as a servant, and the like; and of you and of us, in all these respects fidelity and integrity will be required.

We must indeed abstain from many things which you may do, or at least which you do. But, either these things are in and of themselves bad, or they are not. Be they in and of themselves bad; then have you as little right and leave to do or to use them, as we; and they are not to be excused by any distinction between clergyman and laic. Poison

Poison will ever remain poison, let who will find pleasure in taking it. But are these things not bad, and we yet refrain from them; we then do so out of respect to certain prevailing prejudices, which cannot perhaps be directly opposed or despised without harm; we do it, that we may not give offence to the weak; we do it, that, by our total abstinence in these respects, we may probably prevent still greater abuses, and at least evince, by our example, that a man may deprive himself of them, and yet be contented and happy.

In fine, we must by all means set a good example to others; and when it really happens, that people believe our doctrines and follow our precepts, we are certainly to be very careful to testify to all men by our whole behaviour, that we believe these doctrines ourselves, and acknowledge these precepts to be right and good. For the rest, we have these duties to observe in common with all you. No man is to give offence or difpleafure to another. Every one muft let the light of his virtue fhine before men. We muft all mutually excite one another to good works. Our example can, however, never be fo extenfive and inftructive as yours. Our mode of life is too uniform. Our connections and bufineffes are not fufficiently diverfified. Hence it is, that the notion that we do many things barely on account of our office, which otherwife we fhould not do, often deprives our beft examples of all their efficacy. How frequently is it faid, when we do any thing tolerably good, "Yes, this he does becaufe he is a clergyman; if fuch perfons did not do fo, who fhould?" We are no more than common chriftians, who cannot be expected to carry our chriftian perfection to fuch a length; nothing of this fort is to be expected of us! How often is it faid: "Yes, he muft needs do fo, or abftain from this, if he will do honour to his profession, if he would not contradict himself. Were it not for this consideration, were he not restrained by fear, were he in our place, he would behave in a very different manner!" Thus do prejudice and partiality but too often enfeeble the influence of our example. With you this is not the case. Your good example is unimpeded and complete in its effects. When the merchants give proofs of great probity and conscientiousness; when the opulent and the noble are modest and humane, and shew by their conduct how little their outward advantages avail in their eyes, and how little he that is poor and lowly is therefore to be scorned; when the man of the world, or the layman as he is called, testifies a reverence for God and religion, and men can discern his unfeigned piety; when any one, who, in respect of his fortune, might indulge in luxury and magnificence, and revel in all kinds of amusements, yet lives in a becoming and orderly manner,

manner, and moderates himself in the enjoyment of sensible pleasures; when persons blooming with the charms of youth and beauty seek to distinguish themselves, not by childish ostentation and vanity, but by wisdom and virtue, displaying indeed an open countenance and a chearful spirit, but no senseless and frivolous behaviour: this, Sirs, it is this that strikes a far deeper impression on all beholders, than most of our discourses and actions can do.

Hitherto we have been encountering prejudices no less hurtful than common. We shall now find it so much the easier to delineate the subject before us according to its natural features and complection. If therefore this be not the relationship in which the preacher stands towards his congregation, what then ought it to be, and what actually is it?

First,

First, he should be the teacher of the people, or of the congregation. Certainly a very honourable, but at the same time a very difficult employment! How important are the matters he has to teach; and how much depends upon the way and manner in which he teaches them! He should be a teacher of religion, and of generally useful wisdom. As a teacher of religion, he must instruct his hearers in the regards wherein they stand towards God, their creator and preserver, their father and benefactor, their lawgiver and judge, and towards Jesus Christ, his son, their redeemer and lord. He must furnish them with adequate and worthy conceptions of the majesty and perfections of God, of his protection and love towards men, of the sanctity and justice of his laws, of the wisdom and goodness of his providence, and of the benefits he has been graciously pleased to grant us by Jesus and his work on earth. He is to tell them how God is

disposed

disposed towards them; what he requires of them; what they have to hope or to fear from him according to the difference of their conduct; whereto they are appointed in the present and in the future world; and what they must do for being and becoming what, according to the gracious purpose of God, they ought to be and to become. He must shew them how they are to apply the doctrines of religion to themselves; how they are to use them in all the events of life; how they are to fight with them against temptations to sin; to facilitate the practice of goodness to them, to exalt their taste for the comforts and satisfactions which God has permitted them to enjoy, and to render the hardships and burdens supportable which he lays upon them. He therefore must chiefly labour to improve and to calm them; to incite them to the abhorrence of all ungodly behaviour and all worldly lusts, and to a temperate, just, and godly life; inform them of their

affinity

affinity and duties towards each other, and strive to animate them with kind, beneficent and brotherly difpofitions towards all their fellow-chriftians and mankind. He muſt form them into good and public-fpirited citizens, peaceful and loving fpoufes, faithful fathers and mothers of families, affectionate friends, and fincere worſhipers of God. He is to teach them confcientiousnefs in their dealings, humility and temperance in profperity, patience in tribulations, hope and chearfulnefs in death. In ſhort, he muſt guide them on the way of virtue and religion to tranquillity of mind, to continued advances in perfection and happinefs. Thus will a preacher declare to his hearers the whole counfel of God to their felicity. Thus will he preach to them Jefus Chriſt, and him crucified, that is, the doctrine of Jefus Chriſt the crucified, in oppofition to the Jewiſh expectations of a worldly Meſſiah, and the idolatrous doctrines of the heathens. A doc-

trine

trine which is of a large and indefinite comprehension, and which certainly precludes nothing that has a tendency to enlighten and improve mankind.

No: as often as I preach such truths as tend to promote human perfection and happiness; the truths that have a practical influence on the moral behaviour, and on the repose and resignation of mankind; so often do I preach Jesus, and him crucified; so often do I contribute to carry on his work on earth; so often do I proportionately supply his place among my brethren. For he came, he lived, he taught, he suffered and died, he arose again from the dead, and is now the head and the lord of his church, for disseminating truth, and virtue, and happiness among the human race; and whatever advances them is his work, is consistent with his aims, enlarges and confirms his kingdom; though it be, as it were, not immediately connected with his

his hiftory, nor exprefsly contained in fuch of his difcourfes as are come down to us. As unchangeable as truth is in itfelf; fo little will it allow its extent and the manner of its delivery to be fixed and eftablifhed for all times, and for all mankind. Each age, each fociety of men, has its own horizon, its own circuit of comprehenfion, its peculiar exigencies, its peculiar obftacles, and means of affiftance; and the teacher of religion muft govern himfelf accordingly, if he be determined to do his duty, fo far as his frailty allows him, and refolutely do that which Jefus or his Apoftles would have done, had they been placed in his fituation.

The teacher of religion muft therefore alfo be a teacher of wifdom in a general fenfe. He muft deliver to his hearers, and particularly to the youth he inftructs, not only the peculiar doctrines of religion, but muft likewife fubjoin fuch other ufeful knowledge as either leads to the knowledge of religion, and gives a kind of foundation to it, promotes and settles it, or else may contribute to the repose and improvement of men. And here but too often do persons make false representations of the office and appointment of the christian teacher. They take it amiss, they even impute it to him as a sin, if he do not frequently, if he do not constantly discourse on the mysteries, as they are called, of christianity; that is, of things which we either do not understand at all, or whereof we have, at most, but an extremely feeble glimpse. It is taken amiss, if he do not continually inforce the peculiar articles of faith, as they are termed, if he annex to them a variety of ideas as unavoidable as harmless, and does not account every error as dangerous to a man as every vice. It is called in derision philosophical and moral preaching, when we discourse of the nature and destination of man, of the real value of

the

the possessions, and satisfactions, and occupations of this life, if we speak of separate duties and virtues, of their influence on our present happiness, of the arguments which even sound reason affords for the fulfilling of these duties and the practice of these virtues, and of the way and manner by which we are to fulfill and practise them in every ocurrence. But how unjust are these reproaches! Is not reason then a gift and a revelation of God? Is not every truth in perfect harmony with itself? What value then can a blind implicit faith possess? Of what consequence is a faith without works? A religion without morality? Is not this the scope of that? Is it not the aim of all religion to make us wiser and better? And is any thing to be rejected that promotes this end? Can the foundation of our virtue and our hopes be too deeply laid, or too firmly settled?

No; the preacher is for the generality of men, according to the present state of things, the proper public teacher of expedient wisdom; and to maintain this character must be at once both his endeavour and his glory. By his means must such men as have no other opportunities of instruction, be brought to rational reflection, to the better use of their mental faculties, to greater attention to moral, invisible, and distant objects; by his interposition must all prevailing prejudices and errors be combated, which have a noxious influence on the conduct and serenity of men, the most philosophical knowledge be ever farther spread, and by little and little, the sum of truths which every one knows and adopts, be incorporated into one common stock. He must, however, so contrive to deliver what he has to say in a manner adapted to the comprehension of the unlettered mind, and to this end he must not use the language of the dogmatists or of the

the schools, but the language of common life in use among well-educated and good-mannered men. Let him do this; let him be thus at once a teacher of religion and of wisdom: and he will certainly so much the more contribute to the improvement and happiness of mankind. To promote and to further this is the whole of his duty; and whatever has a tendency thereto is consistent with his office and his calling.

The preacher must, secondly, be the mediate person by whom the congregation are conjoined in their public worship, and the various acts of it collectively performed. There must be order in every society; and when certain matters are to be done collectively, then one of the society must take the lead; he must be the organ by which the rest express their sentiments, their desires, their joys, their hopes, and the like. And this the pastor, or the preacher, is. He performs the different acts

acts of public worship; he reads the Scriptures, utters the prayers, and delivers such instruction as is adapted to the circumstances and exigencies of the community. He is, as it were, their mouth, when they confess their sins before the sovereign judge of the world; when they humble themselves in the presence of his majesty, and implore his grace; when they flee to him for succour, thank him for his bounties, and renew their protestations of obedience. He unites himself with the whole society of the worshipers of God in these pious dispositions and feelings; and strives so to express himself in his exhortations as may best contribute to raise and support their attention. In like manner, as minister, he admits members, by baptism, into the fellowship of the Christian church; and, on these occasions, admonishes the rest of what they are as christians, and what they ought to be; to remember alway that baptism doth represent unto us our profession, feffion, which is to follow the example of our Saviour Chrift, and to be made like unto him; that as he died and rofe again for us, fo fhould we, who are baptized, die from fin, and rife again unto righteoufnefs, continually mortifying all our evil and corrupt affections, and daily proceeding in all virtue and godlinefs of living. So likewife does he adminifter the rite of the Holy Communion; and, in the place of the father of the family, diftributes the bread and the wine among thofe that prefent themfelves with him at table; exhorting them to take and eat in remembrance that Chrift died for them, and to feed on him in their hearts by faith with thankfgiving; to drink of the cup in remembrance that Chrift's blood was fhed for them, and to be thankful; thus directing their thoughts and their hearts to the awful concerns of this folemn celebration. But he performs all this, as, I have

have already obferved, not as a perfon by whofe interpofition our acts of devotion can acquire a greater value, or our facred rites a peculiar efficacy, independent on the fentiments and piety of the faithful partaker; but he does it, becaufe order and the common edification require that certain perfons fhould be ordained to the performance of this folemnity, and becaufe he is commiffioned to do it by lawful authority.

Laftly, the preacher is alfo to be the friend and the counfellor of his flock. If the Chriftian preacher were or could be more fo, he certainly might do more good in his ftation. But he can only be fo as far as his congregation will allow him. No man can force himfelf upon any as their friend or their counfellor; and if a perfon fhould attempt it, he would by that very means fail of the purpofe he had in view. At the fame time, the teacher muft be be always ready to embrace such opportunities as naturally offer, and use them with fidelity. It need hardly be mentioned, that he is not to interfere in extraneous matters, or misapply the respect which accrues to him either from his office or his personal qualities, to the prosecution of selfish views, or the gratification of disorderly passions. As a teacher, he is only to meddle with moral and religious objects, and with the application of them to particular events and occurrences of life. Since he may reasonably be presumed to have reflected on these matters more, and to be more intimately acquainted with them, than the generality of his hearers; and, as in his public discourses pronounced to a very mixt assembly, he cannot say every thing it were profitable and necessary for any one in particular to know; it would certainly be of great utility, if opportunities were afforded him to fupply this unavoidable defect of inftruction by private converfation. By this channel might he convey direction and affiftance to him who fhould be defirous of making farther progrefs in the knowledge of religion : thus might he deliver the candid and ingenuous doubter from his doubts, or tranquillize him in them : thus might he remove many a prejudice from the anxious and perturbed mind, and bring the forrowful heart to a comfortable and joyful reliance on the Gofpel : thus might he be enabled to fpeak courage to the fincere but feeble chriftian, and probably facilitate to him the conqueft of himfelf and the world : thus might he inform any individual how he muft apply to himfelf and his particular circumftances the general precepts and encouragements of religion. So would the teacher be at the fame time the leader and the counfellor of his flock; and fo might he likewife, in a ftricter a stricter sense, be said to watch over their souls, and labour more effectually at their improvement and felicity.

And this, Sirs, is the relationship wherein the preacher stands towards his congregation: he is their teacher, their leader, their friend, and adviser. Allow me to conclude this discourse with drawing a few consequences from what has been said, and reminding you of the duties which in this respect you are bound to preserve.

You plainly perceive from all that has been advanced, that we, preachers, require of you no blind faith, no servile obedience, no unlimited occurrence. We feel our infirmities and frailties much too sensibly to pretend to this; and the more we are animated by the spirit of Christianity, the more zealously shall we in these respects maintain the cause of freedom.

No;

No; try all things that are taught you for truth, and enjoined you as duties: compare them with what reason and scripture tell you of God and his will; prove all things, and adhere to that which is good. The more carefully we examine our doctrines, the more you reflect upon them; the more you discourse with each other about them, in honest intentions; so much the greater are our hopes that you will reap benefit from them. Only by such reflections, only by such examinations and discussions, can what we tell and teach you assimilate itself with your own system of reflection, and either rectify or enlarge it.

You see, farther, that we require no excessive and superstitious reverence from you. The office we bear is undoubtedly honourable, and they that bear it must be held in a certain degree of estimation, if their bearing of it is to be attended with success.

success. When, therefore, you spare us; when you conceal as much as possible our failings and imperfections from the consideration, lest the respect to our office should thereby be lessened, and the useful effects of it be hindered; you then act wisely, and in consistence with your duty. For the rest, judge of us, with the same equity and philanthropy, you are accustomed to use in judging of your neighbours in general; and let us experience the same justice and lenity that is due to all mankind.

You see, thirdly, in what regard we properly stand towards you. Require, therefore, no more from us than you may accordingly, and with reason expect. Require neither supernatural gifts and powers, nor a perfection that is above the reach of humanity. Ascribe no greater importance to our words and actions, no

greater

greater efficacy than they really possess. Rely not upon us in matters, where no man ought or can rely upon another; where every man must provide for himself and his own concerns. Think not that we either can or ought to do the most in number or in consequence of the things that relate to the salvation of your soul and your everlasting happiness. No; it is our part to shew you what, in this respect, you have to do; and the latter is incontestably far more important and difficult than the former. Seek not therefore to rid yourselves of any imputations, by throwing charges upon us, for which you alone must be responsible; and constantly bear in mind the expressions of the apostle: " Every man shall bear his own burden; " Every one of us shall give an account of " himself to God."

Lastly, you see how weighty and arduous our ordination is. Alleviate then, as much

as

as you can, the concerns and duties of it; alleviate them to us by the attention you afford to our difcourfes; by the zeal and devotion with which you frequent all the rites of the public worfhip; by the vigilant infpection you keep over your children whom we inftruct; by the encouragements you give them; by the converfations you hold with them on what they are learning, and what they have already been taught; by the application you make of it to the cultivation of their heart, and the forming of their conduct. In a more efpecial manner, lighten to us the burden of our office, and reward us for our pains by the faithful ufe you make of our doctrine; by the willing obedience you pay to our well-founded admonitions and exhortations; by the good deeds which you perform; by the fhining virtues by which you diftinguifh yourfelves from others; by your continual improvement in wifdom and piety. This will be an ample teftimony that our labours in

your

your behalf have not been in vain; and this assurance will render all the efforts and toils we exert and undergo, easy and pleasant. It will never allow us to become either faint or weary; and even in the hour of death, and at the day of judgment, it will be our comfort and joy.

THE END.

www.ingramcontent.com/pod-product-compliance
Lightning Source LLC
Chambersburg PA
CBHW032033220426
43664CB00006B/454